Facilitating Interpersonal Relationships in the Classroom

The Relational Literacy Curriculum

Facilitating Interpersonal Relationships in the Classroom

The Relational Literacy Curriculum

Diane Salmon, PhD
Ruth Ann Freedman, EdD
National-Louis University

 LAWRENCE ERLBAUM ASSOCIATES, PUBLISHERS
2002   Mahwah, New Jersey   London

Lawrence Erlbaum Associates, Inc., Publishers
10 Industrial Avenue
Mahwah, NJ 07430

Cover design by Kathryn Houghtaling Lacey

Library of Congress Cataloging-in-Publication Data

Salmon, Diane.
The relational literacy curriculum : creating connections in the classroom / Diane Salmon and Ruth Freedman.

    p. cm.

    Includes bibliographical references and index.
ISBN 0-8058-3764-7 (cloth : alk. paper)
ISBN 0-8058-3765-5 (pbk. : alk. paper)
1. Social skills—Study and teaching (Elementary).   2. Social learning.   I. Freedman, Ruth (Ruth Ann).   II. Title.
HM691 .S35 2001
372,6 —dc21   2001025855
                                                            CIP

Books published by Lawrence Erlbaum Associates are printed on acid-free paper, and their bindings are chosen for strength and durability.

Printed in the United States of America
10 9 8 7 6 5 4 3 2 1

To our children
Daniel, Alec, Rachel, and Hannah
and the friendships they'll encounter.

Contents in Brief

Contents

Preface

The story behind this text, *Facilitating Interpersonal Relationships in the Classroom: The Relational Literacy Curriculum*, actually began in the spring of 1993. Ruth, a teacher with over seven years of teaching experience, a master's degree, and some further educational work, found herself with a group of third grade girls who were struggling through a wide range of complex social issues within their friendships. Ruth luckily made a connection and future partnership with her colleague Diane, a professor of educational psychology with experience working with children on social problem solving. Together, with the help of many children at Baker Demonstration School, colleagues at the school, graduate students of National-Louis University and other teachers, we have researched, inquired and developed the Relational Literacy Curriculum.

The timeliness of this curriculum is evident in recent literature of the fields of psychology and education that has emphasized the importance of preventing social conflict through activities that promote social understanding and communication skills. Consistent with this prevention theme, the Relational Literacy Curriculum is designed to be integrated into the elementary classroom curriculum in order to elaborate children's understanding of relationships and provide a resource for managing conflict within the classroom community. The Relational Literacy Curriculum uses stories of relational dilemmas as a means of engaging children in reflective discussions and role plays to explore the dynamics of relating.

This book is a guide for implementing the Relational Literacy Curriculum (RLC), a conceptual framework and method for enhancing children's understanding of interpersonal relationships in the classroom. The RLC is intended for use with children in the second through fifth grades. Based upon developmental and social constructive principles, the design of the curriculum encourages children to reflect upon challenging interpersonal episodes and to discern constructive patterns of relating through discussion and role playing. The curriculum process can be an excellent tool for addressing conflict as well as promoting classroom community. In this way, it is both a tool to address immediate interpersonal conflict and one to reduce the likelihood of future conflict. Although written primarily for classroom teachers, school psychologists, school counselors, and social workers will find this book useful in their efforts to enhance children's social understanding during the elementary years. Teacher educators will also appreciate this book as a resource for courses and workshops on classroom management, clinical practica, and student teaching seminars.

OVERVIEW

In the organization of this book, we weave together a strong conceptual grounding with a set of practical classroom strategies. Chapters 1 and 2 provide a broad conceptual overview of the RLC. In chapter 1, we define relational literacy and discuss the significance of studying relationships in the elementary classroom through the use of an actual classroom vignette. In chapter 2, we introduce the broad conceptual framework of the RLC by discussing the theoretical and research literature that ground it. Chapters 3, 4, 5, and 6 deal with specific components of the curriculum. Each includes an action framework for guiding decisions during implementation. In chapter 3, we focus on the RLC discussion process. We offer a framework for discerning the quality of RLC discussions, including examples of children's explanations and teacher prompts. Chapter 4 addresses the role play component of the RLC. We share a developmental framework for understanding children's role play performances, and suggest specific ways of scaffolding their participation and reflection. Chapter 5 discusses activities that allow children to take more responsibility for directing the RLC. Here, we emphasize the importance of using children's own language to make conceptual connections explicit. Chapter 6 explores the use of children's actual conflicts in the context of the curriculum. We share examples from our experiences and highlight the kinds of issues that may be explored. Chapter 7 closes the book with reflections on how teachers can use the RLC to enhance their own professional learning and development. The appendix includes brief summaries of each aspect of the curriculum as well as easy to use worksheets and other tools to aid in implementing the process.

We believe that the conceptually strong design of the RLC, as well as the conceptual emphasis throughout this book, make it a very flexible tool. The RLC design allows teachers to adapt the curriculum to the specific social needs of their classroom contexts and also to effectively improvise as they implement it. Particularly important features of this flexibility are the action frameworks. They allow teachers to work from and build upon a theory, while integrating their own procedures in meaningful ways. Thus, teachers can make use of the RLC according to their own needs.

ACKNOWLEDGMENTS

We wish to thank those who have been important participants in the development of this curriculum. The children who have worked with the curriculum have been treasured gifts to us; the greatest thanks go to them for working with the curriculum during various stages of development. For over five years, the children in Ruth's second and third grade classroom at Baker Demonstration School at National-Louis University helped us as we developed the RLC, sharing their friendship stories, their real relational conflicts, and so much more. We have learned much in listening to them and each chapter begins with a story

or quote from these children. In the fall of 1998, the third graders at Fairview Elementary School helped us to extend the curriculum. During the 1999–2000 school year, the children in Juli
Ross's fourth grade class at Baker Demonstration School
helped to refine the curriculum, most especially the role playing.

With each new group of children, other individuals, mainly
National-Louis University students and colleagues, worked with
us and helped to refine the curriculum. We wish to thank each of
them for their personal contribution to our book. Debbie Ander-
son, Leslie Golhooley, and Peggy McCarthy helped us in the initial stages of the work. Sue Klein helped to interview students
and developed her own thesis on our work. As part of a small research grant through the Spencer Foundation, we implemented
the curriculum with three Elementary School teachers: Brooke
Ebner, Bernadette Gonzalez, and Cheryl Griffin. We wish to
thank the foundation for their financial support and the teachers for the many contributions they made to the RLC, particularly issues of implementation in chapter 3. Juli Ross and
Lizanne Wilson of Baker worked with us to refine the curriculum with older students and to explore role play. Juli was particularly instrumental in piloting several new role play formats.

During the past seven years, we received support from the
administration at National-Louis University. Linda Tafel, pro-
vost, and David Freitas, our dean, encouraged us throughout
this time period with financial and emotional support as well
as release time for research and writing. The institution supported us through our sabbaticals during the 1997–98 academic year, when we were given time to analyze our research
data. Other colleagues have provided feedback along the way.
We thank Diane Deckert, Sheila Eller, Jill Brodkowitz,
Meredith Sinclair, and Krista Robinson who all experimented
with the curriculum. Dr. Becky Barr read and provided feedback on papers related to the RLC.

A special thanks goes to Chris Fogartaigh who authored
chapter 4 and has worked with us on the curriculum since
1997. He has worked with various teachers with the RLC and
made many important contributions. His work on the role play
is critical to the successful implementation of the RLC. Our
friend and colleague, Mary Jane Eisenhauer, was generous and

kind with her time as she helped to revise and edit this text. As a classroom teacher and researcher, her insights have been critical to this book.

We also want to thank our families and friends who have supported us along the way and helped us understand the nature of relationships. A special thanks to our parents, Arlene and Ken Freedman, and Doris and Bob Salmon, who nurtured our earliest relationships; Marty Rosenheck who early on recognized the importance of our work with children and encouraged us as we formulated our research into a book; and Dan Wander, Ruth's husband and best friend, who helped us make this book a priority, always knowing it would be published. Finally, we celebrate the opportunity to work together and build and nurture our own friendship which has been the greatest benefit of the RLC.

List of Tables

List of Figures

1

Relationships: Why Study Them in the Elementary Classroom?

MARK'S STORY: ONE CHILD'S SOCIAL CONFLICT

Mark is having trouble with one of his friends. Mark is confused. He doesn't know what to do. He steals all of Mark's
food at lunch, and by the time Mark gets it back there is
hardly enough time for Mark to eat his lunch. He even gets
Mark's other friends to go along with him, except Don.
Telling him to lay off and quit picking on Mark doesn't
work. He is pushing Mark to the limit. Mark has reasoned
with him, talked to him, and now he even punched Mark in
the chest very hard six or seven times. Now Mark wants to
get revenge on his friend. Mark wants his friend to be trans-
ferred to another class. Mark wants to hurt his friend's feelings the same way, as Mark's feelings have been hurt.
(Child-authored story of class episode)

Mark's mother, Jackie, a working parent, arrives in her son's
classroom just before school begins, feeling an important need to
share the story of her son's difficult experience in school the previous day. In Mark's second–third-grade classroom, where peer
relationships and social interactions are valued, such parent–
teacher occurrences are not unusual. Conversations like this oc-

1

cur on a daily or weekly basis with concerned parents. Mark's teacher understands and values the idea that schooling is a partnership between home and the larger school community. In this particular instance, it is clear to the teacher from observing the mother's demeanor and expression that as a parent she is particularly troubled by the interactions that have occurred between her son and the other boys. Jackie has been attempting to provide support at home for her son to help him resolve this dilemma. She has spoken with her son, supported his feelings and tried to follow the normal guidelines.

Mark is a third-grade boy with healthy, normal, fluid relationships within his multi-age classroom. He is a child who is well-liked by his peers and interacts socially and academically with a wide range of other children. Over the two-year period Mark has been a student in this same classroom, this is the first social issue about which his mother has come to speak with the teacher. As an involved and committed parent, she is appropriately concerned because her son has been bothered by this set of particularly troubling social interactions within the classroom community for a week and she can no longer provide answers for him. These relational issues have evolved into a very complex dynamic and Mark is now unmotivated to come to school and appears not to be able to focus on academic tasks. Mark's emotional response about his social relationships have become so acute that it is all he can focus on when he discusses school with his mother. Mark's mother is seeking advice and guidance from the teacher about this dilemma. Jackie is aware that in the classroom relational issues are valued in the same manner academic issues are. She needs support for her child and believes the classroom teacher possesses an expertise to facilitate solutions for this issue. Jackie arrives at school on this particular day ready to collaborate with the teacher to resolve this problem.

Although Mark's mother has been effective in supporting and mediating other social conflicts, this problem has reached a level of complexity that demands more. It demands a process that includes all the involved children in a constructive way. A process that doesn't seek to punish, but instead offers opportunities for learning. A process that doesn't focus on blaming, but instead invites reflection on personality characteristics and their implications for relating. A process that doesn't give children the right answer, but instead encourages them to construct their own language and build a framework for organizing their actions and reactions within complex dynamic social events. As is the typical procedure in this classroom when complex social conflicts arise, the teacher suggests that Mark and his mother co-construct a story about the problem he is experiencing. Jackie feels good about the fact that the classroom problem-solving process will be utilized to work through her son's problem, and leaves prepared to facilitate the writing of a story with her son.

Mark returns to school the following day with his carefully written story ready to present it to the other boys involved in the conflict. He is feeling better about returning to school because he knows a process to resolve the social conflict is underway.

The Relational Literacy Curriculum (RLC), a curriculum that addresses conflict through discussion and role play, is this process. In taking this approach, the teacher has given control of the situation to Mark and the other students and thus Mark feels more secure about the outcome. The teacher has not solved the problem for Mark or the other children, but rather provided a forum for the problem to be explored. Even the students in the class are aware of the process available in the classroom to resolve this conflict.

Teacher:	Mark came to me on Monday with a big problem. So who thinks that they know what I might have done and said to Mark.
Child:	Get us and tell us to come at 1:30 p.m. today.
Teacher:	And what did he do?
Child:	He wrote a story.

Mark invites all of the children he feels are directly and indirectly involved in the story to work through the social problem-solving discussion process. In sharing his story, Mark states that "he steals all of Mark's food and even gets others to go along." In the problem-solving discussion that ensues, the boys work through the dilemma by exploring the nature of the problem, who is involved, why they think it is happening, and how they will resolve it.

Teacher:	What's the problem?
Child:	That somebody is hurting Mark.
Child:	Very badly.
Teacher:	Okay, Mark is being hurt. Is he being hurt both physically and emotionally?
Child:	Yes.
Teacher:	Okay, you know the difference between those, right?
Children:	Yes.
Teacher:	Is it equally valid to be hurt? Is it equally painful to be physically hit as being emotionally hurt?
Children:	Yes.
Child:	Depends on which one, you could get like, matters how bad.
Child:	Well, it depends on which one is worse, you could get like really bad hurt feelings like Mark.
Child:	Or paralyzed legs or something.

As the children examine the story through discussion, they simultaneously explore some important issues about human experience and the nature of relationships. In this exploration, they gain mental and emotional distance from the episode in which they were involved, which may free them to see new avenues for action. Through constructive group dialogue on social issues, a greater sense of community is also fostered. The dialogue provides an opportunity for the group to evolve a shared language for referencing relational dynamics.

A central goal of this volume is to share the curriculum process that we have used to aid children's understanding of social relationships and relational tensions. Mark and his peers in the incident described previously would not have been as prepared to explore their real dilemma had they not been participating in an ongoing curriculum involving the exploration of hypothetical problems. Through this curriculum, the children create shared resources to aid their development of relationships within the classroom community. In sharing our curriculum process, we also describe the nature of these resources that include not only individual knowledge and skills, but also the less tangible language processes involved in creating classroom cultures. We turn now to hear the teacher's side of the story.

A TEACHER'S STORY: ONE TEACHER'S RESPONSE TO SOCIAL CONFLICT

All elementary classroom teachers to some extent engage in conversations such as the one with Mark's mother and the small group of boys. Through the appearance of real, concrete and difficult social conflicts within classrooms, teachers are requested by children and parents to meet the social–emotional needs of children and to facilitate and mediate social–peer relationships within our classroom communities. The social conflicts are presented in such a manner that teachers, who genuinely care about children, cannot avoid them. They are usually presented at the crisis point, when teachers must provide some assistance for resolving the issue. The reality of classroom life, more than 20 young children residing in a small classroom, requires this assistance. The immediate needs of the children in classrooms demand that teachers mediate relationships in some way or another.

Ruth, Mark's teacher, responded to the dilemma that Mark and his mother presented by using a curricular tool designed to help children learn through and resolve their own social problems. In the past, Ruth may have felt pressured to find a quick fix to the dilemma, to smooth over the issues between the boys, and get back to the business of teaching and learning. Instead, she viewed the incident as an opportunity to learn like many others within her classroom, only instead of math, science, or reading, this one involved the domain of human relationships. In spending time on this as she did, Ruth validated the importance of the children's experiences with their peers and helped them to learn from them.

Ruth holds high expectations for all her students. She believes that each has his or her own strengths and areas of expertise, and strives to support and validate these within the classroom. In particular, she believes that each child brings a wealth of experience with social relationships and that they are capable of offering important insights into relating through well-structured questioning and discussion. In the following dialogue excerpt, the boys continue their discussion of Mark's story by exploring why the problem has been happening.

Teacher:	Okay, I think it is important though for Joe to put that one on here, which is 'Joe is encouraged to do this to Mark.'
Child:	But that doesn't mean he should do it.
Joe:	It is hard, I don't want to get in a, I don't want my friends to, if I don't do it my friends are going to be like, "Oh you wimp or some." I'm afraid.
Teacher:	Does anyone know what that is called?
Child:	Are you saying that?
Teacher:	Does anyone know what that is called?
Child:	That has happened to me.
Child:	Well people have told me when he goes that way, you go get this. And when, if I say no, they will say, like you little wimp, I'm not going to be friends with you anymore.
Teacher:	Okay, does anybody know what that is called when your friends—
Child:	It is kind of like pushing them, like ...
Teacher:	Pushing.
Child:	Like sitting in your ... like cigarette pushers. You know. They think it is not addictive but you can stop when you want to.

In this interaction, we see Ruth validating a child's explanation and eliciting others' thoughts on it. The teacher here assumes that children bring a level of expertise in relating, upon which she can draw and help them to make new connections. This conversation becomes an occasion to scaffold the children in thinking about the more complex topic of peer pressure. The children become aware of how they influence one another, and in the process create novel expressions and metaphors to convey their observations and experiences. Ruth values this ability and encourages the children to use their language as a tool to extend their thinking as well as their development of community.

Over the years that she engaged in the relational literacy process, Ruth developed powerful and substantial ways to help children like Mark who experience the real-life social relational problems we all face in our friendships. In the process, those children with more challenging issues have also found support within the classroom community. As she grew to understand the value of relational literacy, it has been placed in the same place as other forms of literacy. Ruth has given her students the opportunity to experience social interactions, relationships, and friendships as a natural literacy event in the classroom. Stories such as Mark's are part of the daily fabric of the classroom community, and children and parents feel confident that their children are elaborating their understandings about social relationships and interacting with a variety of other individuals and groups.

WHAT IS RELATIONAL LITERACY?

The term relational literacy holds multiple meanings. By relational literacy, we primarily refer to an ability to reflect upon, describe, and negotiate relationships in personally meaningful ways. This is a form of literacy that involves the ability to manipulate the symbols of relationships. A central goal of the curriculum is to support children's evolving literacy in the domain of interpersonal relationships. Simultaneously, we adopted this term to indicate that the exploration of relationships can occur through literacy events common to the elementary classroom. In this way, the RLC is not an add on, one more thing to do in an overcrowded elementary curriculum, but rather another dimension to what is often already occurring. In elementary classrooms, children are frequently listening to stories, discussing and enacting their interpretation of stories, writing their own stories, and using stories to look back at their own worlds. These literacy events are central to the RLC. It is our hope that teachers will build upon what they see in the RLC and evolve their own ways of enhancing children's relational literacy.

The goals of the RLC further elaborate our definition of relational literacy. Specifically, they are:

- To help children elaborate and refine their understandings of friendship and other relationships.

- To help children develop a language with which to share and clarify their social experiences.

- To provide a process through which children can articulate, explore, and critique group norms.

- To foster independent social problem solving strategies.

These goals highlight the importance of both individual and community learning processes. We extend our discussion of these goals in the following chapter as we share the theoretical foundations of the RLC.

The development of the RLC occurred over a seven-year time period in which we learned a great many things about friendship, about ourselves, and about the students we have worked with in the process. Drawing from our different disciplinary backgrounds in psychology and reading, we shared a wide range of educational theorists and collaborated to determine which of these ideas we would incorporate into the RLC. Each year, we refined our thinking and explored a different aspect of the curriculum through an action-research process. At different times, one of us has been the leader within this work, while the other has been a follower. We also shared the curriculum with other teachers to further explore its utility and value. With this effort, we clarified and validated many important aspects of the curriculum, in particular, the nature of the teacher's discourse, and created tools for helping teachers use the framework flexibly within their classroom context. We share these tools throughout the present volume. Through our interdisciplinary collaboration, we developed a broader perspective on curriculum. We have brought in our own discipline and worked hard to honor each other's views. Most importantly, we have learned much about children's friendships in the context of elementary classrooms.

VALUES AND COMMITMENTS IN THE RLC

* Relationships are an important domain of study in the elementary classroom.
* Children have competence from which adults can learn.
* Open dialogue is an important way to learn.
* A sense of community is significant for learning.

Through our various reflections on the RLC, we've surfaced our own values and commitments with regard to teaching and learning. We've also learned that these are important to the successful implementation of the RLC. First, we view relationships as a legitimate, and indeed, important domain of study in the elementary classroom. Students need time to observe and reflect on their social interactions with peers in a way they can learn from it. Punitive responses to children's relational challenges leave little opportunity for learning. Taking time for learning about relationships within the elementary curriculum can actually save time later when problems or issues arise. The groundwork has been laid for community dialogue and problem solving.

Second, we assume that children have a great deal of knowledge and competence with respect to relationships and how they work. Indeed, they are highly competent social learners from whom we all can learn. Their ideas must be accepted and respected. At the same time, children can and do revise their ideas when they encounter other more plausible views and explanations. Children need opportunities to make their knowledge explicit. As they share and examine their social knowledge, it becomes more accessible and useful to them. In addition, through sharing with others, they may come to see aspects of their knowledge that may be limited or faulty. Teachers can use sharing opportunities to highlight useful or constructive ways of viewing an event or interpersonal situation. In this way, they support children in revising and elaborating their own knowledge.

We assume dialogue is an extremely important avenue for learning. Through dialogue children gain conceptual distance from interaction and are able to view it from different perspectives. Language offers children a conceptual tool to analyze and represent complex social dynamics. Over time, classroom dialogues can help children to develop a shared language and a shared oral text from which to view and understand social issues in the group. Talk is an important resource in learning.

Finally, we assume that a sense of community is significant to learning. The time devoted to processes such as the RLC helps teachers build community within their classroom. A strong sense of community better prepares children for working and learning together.

OVERVIEW OF THE RLC

The RLC is a year-long curriculum comprised of weekly 30- to 40-minute classroom meetings (see appendix A). We organize the year of meetings in terms of two large curricular cycles, each encompassing about half of the school year. The basic cycle of the curriculum is completed in the fall semester. In this cycle of the curriculum, the children learn a process for discussing and role playing social dilemmas. They are also introduced to a set of dialectic tensions associated with the communication processes involved in initiating and maintaining friendship and other close relationships (Rawlins, 1992). These include the tensions of judgment–acceptance, independence–dependence, expressive–protective, and instrumentality–affection. In the second half of the year, the teacher further contextualizes the curriculum into his or her classroom depending upon the needs of the group and other ongoing curricular goals and processes. An important aspect of this second cycle is the use of the children's real conflicts in the discussion–role play process. We discuss each of these cycles further.

The Basic Cycle

The initial RLC cycle can be further segmented into four smaller two-week cycles. Week one of a small cycle involves a problem-solving discussion based upon a hypothetical dilemma between friends. The discussion is organized around three main questions (What is the problem? Why do things like this happen? What are some choices?). The major ideas that the children generate are recorded on large chart paper for all to review. In the second week of a cycle, the children engage in role plays based upon some of the explanations and choices that they generated. Following each role play the children reflect upon the role plays by discussing how the interaction worked, what might happen, and what would really work. The social dilemmas in each brief story that the children discuss illustrate one of the four dialectic tensions previously mentioned (and described more fully in the following chapter), so that each of the four small cycles focuses on a different tension. Following the four discussion–role-play cycles the children spend two sessions reflecting on the four stories, in order to abstract similarities and differences and to explicitly examine each of the four relational tensions.

The Contextualizing Cycle

The second RLC cycle begins in the second half of the school year. The exact format varies depending on the teacher's preferences, goals, and the needs of the students. The purpose of this second cycle is to give children practice in reflecting on the dialectic tensions as a framework for understanding and communicating effectively in relationships. The children have just been introduced to this framework, so they now need additional opportunities to recognize and apply it. At this point, we often involve the children in writing stories that reflect one of the tensions, and represent events that they have observed or experienced. Alternatively, children can be asked to link the tensions framework to relationships depicted in literature that they are reading. We encourage teachers to think creatively about how they wish to further integrate discussions of relational qualities and challenges into their classroom. At this point in the curriculum cycle, teachers may wish to systematically reflect upon the quality of the relationships in the classroom and how best to focus their energies in the second cycle.

One of the most important ways in which the children can continue to develop their thinking about relationships is to use the RLC process to address real dilemmas as they arise. In so doing, children quickly see how they can apply the problem-solving process and the tensions framework to help them work through real conflict. In supporting them with these real conflicts, teachers help children bridge the knowledge gained in the hypothetical discussions to the real world. Such bridging does not always occur automatically, but must be skillfully scaffolded by the teacher.

OVERVIEW OF THE VOLUME

In the remaining chapters in the volume, we further explain the RLC, both conceptually and practically. In chapter 2, we elaborate upon the values and commitments associated with the curriculum by reviewing the theory and research underlying it. Chapters 3, 4, 5, and 6 discuss some essential procedures for implementing the curriculum. Each chapter also provides an action-oriented framework to help teachers make implementation decisions. We have tried to create a balance between frameworks and procedures in order to provide guidance while allowing teachers the freedom to adapt the curriculum to the culture of their classrooms. Chapter 3 explores the RLC problem-solving discussion providing a framework for monitoring both child explanations and teacher queries. Chapter 4 discusses the role-play process. Chapter 5 describes different ways to help children create conceptual connections across the curriculum. Chapter 6 explores ways in which children's real conflicts can be addressed. In chapter 7, we provide a summary of the RLC focusing on the implementation frameworks and how teachers can make the curriculum their own. We also further explore the concept of community building through the RLC and discuss the benefits of teachers collaborating to engage children in the RLC across multiple years in elementary school. The appendices provide a quick reference in the form of diagrams and worksheets for both the action-oriented frameworks and suggested implementation procedures of the RLC.

2

A Conceptual Framework for the Relational Literacy Curriculum

"There's a whole lot of room in friendship ..."

INTRODUCTION

The RLC cannot be fully implemented without a strong understanding of the broad conceptual framework organizing it. Teaching from a strong conceptual model allows teachers to improvise and adapt the curriculum in principled ways. As the curriculum is flexibly implemented within a particular classroom context, it becomes stronger in the sense that it better addresses the needs of all participants and better reflects the culture of relating within that particular community. In working from a strong conceptual model, teachers also take full ownership of the curriculum. It is more likely to become a part of their personal theory of classroom practice.

We devote this chapter to articulating the conceptual framework behind the RLC. This framework encompasses the rationale behind the curricular goals, a social constructivist account of problem solving, and the dialectic tensions associated with friendships and other close relationships. We discuss these three facets of the conceptual model, explaining theory and research related to each.

UNDERSTANDING THE CURRICULAR GOALS

Goal 1: The RLC is designed to help children elaborate and refine their understandings of friendship and other relationships.

Our first goal is based upon the assumption that children operate with their own personal theories of action regarding friendship (Argyris & Schon, 1974; Cantor & Kihlstrom, 1987; Dweck & Leggett, 1988; Heider, 1958; Kelly, 1955). These theories include knowledge of self and other as well as strategies for relating in particular social situations. Indeed, children can have a great deal of insight regarding relationships, and individual motivations and feelings in interpersonal episodes. Often times, however, these insights are not consciously available to them. By reflecting on interpersonal episodes through a discussion process, such as the RLC, children are able to access and give voice to their implicit views. In this process, children can also learn to critique ways of thinking and problem solving by identifying more and less helpful approaches.

A central characteristic of children's theories in the early elementary grades is a growing capacity to adopt alternative points of view and incorporate them into their decision making (Selman, 1980; Selman & Schultz, 1990; Selman, Watts, & Schultz, 1997; Youniss, 1980). This emerging ability allows children to reason more complexly about interpersonal events and affords them greater flexibility in envisioning potential actions. As children discuss and listen to each other they learn about alternative perspectives on events. The RLC provides such an opportunity for children. In doing so, the curriculum encourages children to adopt points of views other then those they may initially hold. In doing so, they refine and reorganize their personal theories of action.

Goal 2: The RLC is designed to help children develop a language with which to share and clarify their social experiences.

An important avenue for the construction of meaning is through dialogue with others (Bruner, 1990; Vygotsky, 1978; Wells, 1989). We assume that an individual' s construction of meaning is largely a social process, and language is an important vehicle in this process. We draw from Vygotsky's theory in viewing language as a tool for the development of higher order thinking. In this regard, he suggested that mental concepts first exist on an interpersonal, social plane within the dialogue and action of practical activities. In a sense, these concepts are shared or socially distributed in the collaborative activities in which individuals engage. Gradually through these interactions, individuals appropriate these concepts as their own, and the concepts move to an intrapersonal, psychological plane. Individuals participating in shared activities form shared ways of thinking, continually nurturing and enriching the culture of their community. In this regard, the discussion process within the RLC offers an important opportunity. The discussion allows individuals in the classroom to evolve a shared language with which to explain and define their relational experiences. This shared language then can lead to shared concepts of complex relational episodes. In this way, children utilize the RLC for the construction of meaning about social relationships with dialogue as the central vehicle.

In our work with children, we have observed that children use the hypothetical stories we discuss as shared reference points for explaining other social conflicts or issues. They become resources within the classroom community to aid their discussion and explanation of other events (Gergen, 1994). The children also sometimes construct novel metaphors or phrases to explain relational experiences. These metaphors function as shared conceptual tools for interpreting and communicating the data of their social experiences (Lakoff, 1993; Lakoff & Johnson, 1980). Children return to the metaphors that have been particularly helpful to them again and again in their problem solving. The stories and the metaphors children construct become shared conceptual tools, and allow for better collaborative problem solving within the classroom community.

Goal 3: The RLC is designed to provide a process through which children can articulate, explore, and critique group norms.

Children in the middle elementary grades become increasingly concerned with issues of acceptance and inclusion in the peer group (Gottman & Mettetal, 1986). They have a vital interest in understanding what kinds of actions are acceptable and what kinds are not. Children in this age range have yet to fully work out the normative expectations for friendships (Duck, Miell, & Gaebler, 1980). They need opportunities to explore what is acceptable behavior, and to play a role in defining these norms within their classroom. The RLC provides a vehicle for children to explore the nature of different social contexts and actions, and their implications for initiating and maintaining relationships. Through these classroom discussions, children can articulate tacit rules for relating in a way that children who are frequently not privy to this knowledge have access. Children have the opportunity to work with specific problems and issues relevant to their own classroom experiences. All members of the classroom community can play a role in developing, questioning, and critiquing these norms.

Goal 4: The RLC is intended to foster independent problem-solving strategies.

The curriculum is organized around a problem-solving process that has been shown to be effective in enhancing children' s social cognition and interpersonal negotiation skills (Adalbjarnardottir, 1992; Calpan et al., 1992; Gettinger, Doll, & Salmon, 1994; Pelligrini & Urban, 1985). Learning a problem-solving process can help children experience a greater sense of control over their relationships. They have a way of thinking through a situation when challenges arise. As children achieve the first three goals of the curriculum, that is, as they elaborate their understanding of relationships, develop language to better articulate their experience, and critique emerging group norms, they are constructing a strong conceptual foundation for independent social problem solving. At the same time, practice with social problem solving provides children with an avenue to achieve a deeper understanding of relationships, develop language, and critique group norms. Through the RLC, social problem solving is not only an end in itself, but also a means to other ends. We elaborate on how we conceptualize this process in the following section.

RETHINKING SOCIAL PROBLEM SOLVING

The core of the RLC involves the use of hypothetical stories depicting problems between friends and classmates. Children explore these problems through three central questions: What is the problem? Why do things like this happen? What are some choices? These questions are not particularly novel, however, we have a unique emphasis on them. First, we emphasize the process of problem construction rather than problem resolution. Through our questioning, particularly the why question, we encourage children to develop a rich representation of the problem situation. Second, we encourage the children's reflection across different story problem types. Through this reflection, we want them to note important themes and distinctions that will elaborate their understanding of friendship and other peer relationships. These two emphases draw from research in cognitive science and constructivist practices as it applies to instruction.

Although given less attention in the social problem-solving literature, one of the more important aspects of this approach may be the time children spend in constructing a problem definition. Cognitive psychology research on the nature of expertise has examined the process experts take in solving problems within their domain of expertise and how these processes differ from the novice in that domain. This research indicates that more experienced individuals spend time during problem solving developing an abstract mental representation of the problem to be solved, one that allows them to more clearly see alternative solution paths (Chi, Feltovich, & Glaser, 1981; Ericsson, & Smith, 1991; Voss,

Greene, Post, & Penner, 1983; Voss, Sherman, Tyler, & Yengo, 1983). Time spent on building a rich problem representation may be particularly important in ill-structured social domains where problem solutions may not be easily agreed upon (Schon, 1993; Voss, Green, et al.; 1983). With this in mind, we have developed the RLC in such a way that the students spend a significant amount of time constructing a problem definition and specifically exploring why a problem occurred.

Table 2.1 contains a group recording notes written during a RLC classroom discussion. These notes illustrate the broad structure we use to discuss dilemmas with children as well as the nature of the children's language and thinking on the characters and events.

The notes reflect a discussion of a hypothetical story about a troubled threesome. This example clearly illustrates the effects of modifying the traditional problem-solving questions. After defining the problem literally, we ask children to think about why the problem may be happening. In this way, children spend time sharing possible interpretations and co-constructing a richer representation of the problem situation. The notes in Table 2.1 illustrate a number of alternative interpretations. The girls interpreted a character in a particular way. They also considered the circumstances or the characters' interactions over time. Additionally, they considered differences in the nature of the relationships between the characters. All these various interpretations deepened and enriched the basic scenario and lead to a more complex narrative about the characters. In this example, the girls spent much more time interpreting the situation than they did in trying to resolve it. The choices, although few, seemed to be particularly powerful ones, reflecting an attempt to balance tensions often experienced in relationships (Rawlins, 1992).

In addition to interpreting a single story in multiple ways, we encourage children to compare and contrast different stories to gain a different kind of perspective. Deep reflection across carefully chosen problems has important cognitive benefits (Kolodner, 1997). When children are encouraged to reflect upon the various dimensions within a specific problem (i.e., each character's actions and point of view, their history of interac-

TABLE 2.1

Group Recording Notes: Hypothetical Problem Around Independence-Dependence Tension

Story

Once there were three really good friends named Jill, Molly, and Ellen. They had been friends for a quite a few years. This year Ellen suddenly started to draw away from Jill and Molly and play with other people. Sometimes Ellen even was mean to Jill and Molly, making them feel that they had done something to hurt her. Jill and Molly felt really confused. They didn't understand why Ellen was moving away from them and why she was mean to them sometimes. They didn't want to lose her friendship, but they didn't know what to do.

What Is the Problem?

– Ellen isn't playing with Jill & Molly anymore.
– Ellen drew away from her friends.
– Ellen is saying mean things sometimes.
– Jill & Molly don't know what to do; don't want to lose her friendship.
– Jill & Molly don't know why; feeling confused.

Why Do Things Like This Happen?

• Ellen is sick of Jill & Molly; tired of them; bored of being with them; tired of playing the same things.
• Jill & Molly were mean to her and didn't realize it; by accident; Ellen thought they did it on purpose; Ellen felt innocent and didn't understand; sometimes people don't realize when they hurt others.
• Had a fight and didn't really make-up; need more than an apology.
• Someone else is sending Ellen mean notes & she thinks it is Jill and Molly; this person wants Ellen all to herself.
• Ellen's relationship with Jill and Molly feels like sisters; feels like they will understand; "they're family, who cares if they're mad, they'll always be there."
• Ellen is a bit older; she feels more mature; thinks Jill and Molly are babyish.
• Someone in Ellen's family is treating her like this (ignoring her).
• Molly and Jill are not really best friends to Ellen; they don't always need to play with her.
• Jill and Molly gang up on Ellen; when they are having fights.
• Ellen is older; she bosses Jill and Molly around.
• Jill and Molly forget about Ellen.

continued on next page

TABLE 2.1 *(continued)*

- Ellen has lost another relationship; she's taking it out on Jill and Molly.
- Jill and Molly are older; they treat Ellen like a baby.
- The friendship between the three isn't the same; Ellen doesn't feel included enough; they don't play with Ellen equally.
- Ellen didn't pass a test in school; embarrassed to tell Jill and Molly.
- Ellen is jealous of Jill and Molly because they spend so much time together.

Choices?

- Jill and Molly make a plan together; one of them tells Ellen "I like you better."
- Ellen explains to Jill and Molly why she is drawing away; "I don't think you realized...."
- Jill and Molly say "I don't think you noticed, but you're being mean to us."

---

tion) they stand to learn important lessons about others, themselves, and emotions within meaningful life contexts. Kolodner (1997) referred to this approach to learning as case-based. Within this approach, individuals learn principles and practices within a particular domain (e.g. interpersonal relationships) by reflection and participation in the actual contexts in which the principles and practices are to be applied. Social problem solving approaches could be similarly viewed. As children reflect upon stories with specific relational problems between peers, they can learn and reflect upon the tacit social rules governing interaction and the communication of thought and emotion in that particular social context. Reflection on different cases for the purpose of making comparisons and contrasts across contexts can facilitate the development of more abstract principles or rules governing interaction within relationships (Salmon & Fenning, 1993). In effect, case-based learning experiences seem to aid learners in organizing their knowledge into effective systems of understanding. That is, experiences that allow them to construct rich representations of novel events.

The discussion of hypothetical situations prepares students to address real issues that arise among friends and classmates. In fact, the real power of the RLC lies in the children's ability to transfer concepts and tools developed in discussions of hypothetical situations to help them articulate their experience and feelings regarding a real emotionally charged event (Salmon & Freedman, 1999). Having experienced the curriculum together, the children have constructed a shared language and are better prepared to reflect on alternative points of view in their own conflicts. In so doing, they can move beyond the initial surface problem definition to explore underlying feelings and concerns of others involved in their real-life conflicts.

Table 2.2 illustrates the group notes taken during a discussion of a real situation between three third-grade girlfriends. The girls began with a fairly concrete description of events that had recently occurred. In this case, the girls agreed that the story they shared about two of the girls physically bothering the third was also their answer to what is the problem. In their response to why this happened, the girls went on to interpret this situation in some very interesting ways. They began with an interpretation of Ann's mental state and character. They also reflected upon their own characteristic ways of interacting with one another. They finally arrived at an interpretation of their relationship that seemed to be at the heart of the matter. The girls shared that they were all worrying about their relationship in different ways and that they failed to directly communicate to each other their feelings and needs. Instead, they engaged in this physical teasing and only succeeded in exacerbating the troubled relationship. They concluded that they needed to find their strength to communicate and to help each other in this difficult process.

The power of the interpretive aspect of the discussion is clearly evident in this example. Had the girls tried to generate solutions on the basis of the initial problem definition, they would likely have remained focused on the single episode. As they further reflected upon why that episode occurred, the girls had an opportunity to mentally step back from the episode and elaborate their understanding of it. Through the support of the process, they were able to find their strength to organize and articulate their experiences and points of view. In looking across the two example

TABLE 2.2

Group Recording Notes: Real Peer Conflict

Story

Betty and Sally bug Ann. Hurt Ann physically. Betty pinched Ann on the bottom yesterday on the way out of the bus. Pinched Ann more than once on the bus. Sally was poking Ann on the bus. Ann didn't say anything loudly. Ann didn't want to say stop.

Why Do Things Like This Happen?

- Ann was down. Others were trying to cheer Ann up.
- We cheer up each other in different ways; not usual.
- Ann didn't mind at first.
- Ann is shy; Didn't say anything; Didn't tell truth at first; Didn't want to make them feel bad.
- Friendship is wearing out; worry about the friendship; feel guilty; don't share feelings when we're having a fight.

Choices?

- Ann says stop.
- Find our strength to talk to each other.
- Betty and Ann talk to each other; share feelings directly and honestly.
- One person helps the other find her strength.

stories, some interesting similarities emerge. The girls came to see the quality of the relationship between the three to be an important issue in both cases. This insight seemed to help the girls focus on direct and honest ways of communication within the threesome to address the relational tensions.

The importance of problem construction, reflection across different stories, and the use of real stories extend the social problem-solving process. Through the structure of the discussion process, we encourage children to spend time developing a rich definition of the problem in the story by eliciting a variety of interpretations from them. Essentially, we ask them to go beyond what the problem is to consider why problems like that occur. In this way, they move beyond the given text to activate their prior knowledge in regard to the characters and events depicted in the episode. In addition, we encourage reflection across different problems to foster mental connections between various episodes and the relational knowledge these problem episodes evoke. After this kind of practice with hypothetical stories, children bring real stories for discussion and reflection. From their prior experience with the hypothetical stories, they are better able to step back, take a broader view, listen to other perspectives and see their own role in the problem. They also gain this greater perspective on friendship dilemmas from learning about the dialectic tensions inherent in the relational conflicts.

PATTERNS OF RELATING
AND THE DIALECTIC TENSIONS

We have developed and organized the stories discussed within the RLC from a dialectical perspective (Bakhtin, 1981; Baxter & Montgomery, 1996; Rawlins, 1992). In brief, this view defines relationships in terms of communicative processes based upon contradictory tensions, such as involvement–privacy and openness–discretion. Relational competence is a matter of negotiating these tensions in a manner that is sensitive to the unique meaning system that has evolved within the context of the relationship. Our aim within the curriculum is to help children become more aware of the tensions they may need to negotiate in initiating and maintaining varieties of friendships. Through the stories we introduce, we hope to highlight common relational tensions and offer children an opportunity to reflect on the processes involved in negotiating relationships.

Rawlins (1992) provided a particularly useful conceptual framework for understanding the tensions inherent in maintaining friendships. Through in-depth interviews with adults, Rawlins identified four dialectic tensions that characterize communications among friends and potential sources of conflict in these relationships. Table 2.3 briefly describes the nature of each of these four tensions.

We have found these four tensions to be particularly helpful ways of characterizing the various challenges that we see children encountering in their peer relationships. We have used these constructs to organize the story problems in the RLC. In this regard, they provide a helpful focus for the hypothetical

TABLE 2.3
Rawlins Dialectic Tensions

Independence–Dependence	Tension between feeling free to pursue one's own interests and remaining available to the other to sustain the relationship.
Expressive–Protective	Tension between communicating one's feelings and needs, and strategically protecting oneself or the feelings of the other.
Judgment–Acceptance	Tension between evaluating and holding the friend to some standards versus largely accepting the friend for who he or she is.
Instrumentality–Affection	Tension between valuing another as a means to an end versus valuing another as an end in itself.

problem episodes that the children discuss. The dialectic of **independence–dependence** highlights the voluntary nature of friendship. It refers to friends' needs to feel free to pursue their individual interests, and simultaneously remain available to each other to sustain the relationship. In the curriculum, problem episodes involving this tension are often about one friend's shifting interests or a friend's concern for the incorporation of new children within the play. The dialectic of **expressiveness–protectiveness** refers to the delicate balance between communicating one's feelings and needs and strategically protecting oneself or the feelings of others. Problem episodes depicting bossy or overly aggressive friends are typical examples of this tension. The dialectic of **judgment–acceptance** refers to the tension between evaluating and holding the friend to some standards versus largely accepting the friend for who he or she is. Episodes that reflect this tension usually involve exclusion, rejection, and teasing. Finally, the dialectic of **instrumentality–affection** describes the tension between spending time with another because of his or her utility versus spending time with another because it was enjoyable to do so. An example of an episode reflecting this tension for middle childhood students involves one friend playing with another only for their toys or their valued skills.

Rawlins (1992) argued that these four dialectic tensions organize and compose ongoing challenges in the practical management of communications among friends. Each tension represents opposing modes of interaction that need constant monitoring and re-negotiation. Drawing on the developmental literature, Rawlins (1992) speculated that these tensions might be displayed and interpreted differently throughout development. In our own work, we have found the tensions to be meaningful to the children providing them a way to talk about different relationships and experiences (Klein, 1999; Salmon & Freedman, 1995, 1997, 1998).

The dialectic tension framework deepens and enriches the problem-solving process the children learn. We reflect not on a random collection of stories, but on ones that come back to a framework emphasizing key dimensions of relating. In this way, children are helped to see recurrent patterns in the way they and others relate. For example, we observed two girls identify a pattern that troubled their friendship in terms of the expressive–protective tension. They began to see how one girl's pattern of relating emphasized expression, while the other's pattern tended toward protection. They recognized the need to let each other know when they felt uncomfortable with these patterns. The tensions' framework offered the girls a language to describe relational issues that were not only difficult to talk about, but often difficult to identify. It moved them away from blaming the other to think more in relational terms. They each saw that they had a role to play. The use of these four dialectic tensions in the curriculum is important in extending the children's thinking beyond a focus on static personality characteristics to focus on ways of interacting and how harmful patterns might be changed.

CONCLUSIONS

The RLC is a valuable learning tool in a number of ways. The children distinguish and practice modes of thinking that are critical to social understanding. The brief stories help children bring to mind their world knowledge and experience in similar episodes. Through sharing and listening to alternative interpretations, the children gain access to a variety of viewpoints about people and ways of relating that can enrich their personal theories of relationships. In addition, we have found that the various stories that we use for discussion become classroom resources (Gergen, 1994). The children refer back to previously discussed stories in making interpretations of new ones. In this way, a classroom can create its own repertoire of shared stories to help children interpret future events. In effect, the process moves beyond an individual experience in learning to create a classroom culture through which relationships can be organized and interpreted. The community then has a means of making explicit and examining tacit and emerging rules for interaction.

The literature related to our curricular goals, the problem-solving process, and the dialectic tensions form a deliberate conceptual framework for the RLC. This conceptual framework informs curricular decisions regarding implementation and assessment. With a strong theoretical framework organizing curricular action, those actions can be flexibly adjusted to meet the demands of a particular context. A strong theoretical framework such as the one described in this chapter can guide a teacher's decisions; therefore allowing her or him to make powerful and informed decisions about social issues within the classroom. Both hypothetical and real emerging story problems provide a context for children's discussion and reflection. In subsequent chapters, we extend the relational literacy conceptual framework and illustrate how it can inform teaching with additional examples of stories, children's reflections, and actual classroom dialogues.

3

The Relational
Literacy Curriculum
Discussion Process:
Exploring How It Works

"If people could read minds, that would never happen ..."

INTRODUCTION

The RLC discussion process is intended to encourage reflection on interpersonal action. The teacher's role is to encourage the children to articulate their ideas. Rather than finding the right answer, the goal is to have a variety of perspectives on the table for examination. Typically the interpersonal interactions discussed are reasonably complex for the age of the children, and the intentions of characters in the stories slightly ambiguous. Through discussion, we want the children to explore the subtleties of interaction, to examine their own assumptions about why people may behave the way they do, and to consider alternative ways to respond. We want them to move beyond simple explanations or pat solutions to consider alternative perspectives and multiple avenues for the characters. This kind of exploratory talk can expand children's understanding of others and themselves. In addition, it provides practice in a way of thinking that can serve them in real-life conflict.

The RLC begins in the fall of the school year with a series of discussions of hypothetical problems in the form of brief stories. In one 30- to 40-minute class discussion, the children discuss a story using the problem-solving format discussed in chapter 2. They then role play the situation in the next 30- to 40-minute session. In this chapter, we focus on the discussion process and how it works.

An important characteristic of the RLC is its inherent flexibility. The curriculum is organized around a framework that provides guidance, yet allows users to design the most important aspects. The stories that are used as the basis for discussion are one of these important aspects. In the following section, we provide example stories and guidance for story design. In this way, teachers may develop stories around events, characters, and contexts that best suit their classroom needs.

Story discussions can move in different ways depending upon the skills and personalities within the group. In the second major section of this chapter, we provide guidelines and examples of the kinds of dialogue that may occur around the RLC relational tensions. Specifically, we offer general criteria for what to look for in a quality discussion as well as a more detailed framework for anticipating the children's explanations for particular tensions. We include examples of useful teacher prompts to illustrate the teacher's role.

DEVELOPING RLC STORIES

Developing fruitful stories for discussion is one of the most important challenges of implementing the RLC. Overly complicated or irrelevant stories can set the stage for either difficult or dull discussions. Alternatively, clear and meaningful situations can prompt thoughtful dialogue and conceptual growth. The following are some general considerations that we have found important when developing stories.

Relevance of the Story

Pay attention to the interpersonal stories that you hear and see in the classroom. Then develop stories around one of the tensions that seem relevant to the classroom dynamics. Discussing a hypothetical story that has parallels to a real relational tension experienced in the group can be extremely helpful to the children. In this way, they have an opportunity to explore possible explanations and action choices that can relate to their reality, yet they maintain a safe emotional distance from the actual relational issues.

Language

Consider the languages and dialects spoken by the children in the classroom. When there are several English as Second Language (ESL) students present, the vocabulary and story complexity should be kept simple and straightforward (i.e., avoid idioms and slang). Also, the names of the characters ought to be familiar to the students, but avoid using names of class members. We try to alternate between male and female characters in the stories or choose names that can be either male or female.

Story Complexity

Keep the story brief and open to interpretation. Don't feel compelled to provide detail or context. The children will fill in the context and intentions of the characters through their dialogue. This openness allows them to surface their assumptions and beliefs, and to hear those of their classmates. Keep the number of characters low (two or three). Too many different characters may make the story confusing or the conflict too complex. Of course, as the children become more skilled and comfortable in discussing conflict, the number of characters can be increased.

DIALECTIC TENSIONS AS THE BASIS FOR CONFLICT IN THE RLC STORIES

A unique aspect of the RLC is its basis in a dialectic orientation to understanding relationships. In this regard, the story content is organized around the relational tensions identified by Rawlins (1992). As we have suggested elsewhere, the benefit of this approach is that it offers a way of examining and discussing the dynamics of interaction. Too often our language reduces interaction to a description of static qualities of the characters. What we strive for throughout the RLC is a focus on the dynamics of relating, in particular, discerning patterns of relating and how to enhance constructive patterns and how to change destructive ones. Therefore, it's important to have a thorough understanding of the dialectic tensions to create stories around them.

Each of the four tensions consists of two poles representing opposing characteristics. From the dialectic orientation, it is important to keep both of these poles in mind in planning and executing interpersonal encounters. For example, in accepting a friend we may also hold them to some standards. Both acceptance and judgment are a part of friendship. The same is true for each of the other tensions. The challenge is determining the unique blend of these qualities in order to maintain equilibrium in our friendships at any point in time. Usually conflict arises because the balance of the tension has shifted and is uncomfortable for one or more of the characters. This is the case in the stories created for discussion in the RLC. A renegotiation of how that tension is handled in the relationship is necessary for the conflict to be resolved. With experience in discussing RLC stories and reflecting upon the tensions in those stories, children can come to identify the relational tensions creating interpersonal problems and target communication processes to improve relating.

Judgment–Acceptance

Judgment–acceptance refers to the dialectic between accepting the other for who he or she is and judging the other based upon some type of criteria. Through our encounters with others we gradually evolve our standards for judging and accepting within relationships. Rawlins (1992) argued that this is a particularly salient tension in childhood relationships as children explore and develop criteria of their own for acceptable interactions outside the home.

Children in the middle elementary years (second through fifth grade or so) are in the midst of developing standards that are responsive to the needs and interests of others. Early on, children's friendship choices may be based on self-centered needs, superficial features of others, or both. Gradually, they evolve an ability to collaboratively develop evaluative standards with others based upon a desire to foster equality within the relationship (Selman, 1980; Youniss, 1980). The developmental significance of stories organized around this tension, then, is to help children examine their reasons for forming friendships with certain individuals and their reasons for excluding others. We want children to become aware of the standards they hold for others and to consider alternatives. Some children may not have very clear standards and accept anything from their peers. Alternatively, others may be overly restrictive in what they accept, needing to be more accepting and inclusive.

The stories we have used to elicit discussion around the tension between acceptance and judgment within relationships typically involve one child questioning his or her position relative to a group of classmates. Table 3.1 contains some of the hypothetical stories that we have used. Most stories were set in a recess context. One was set in the classroom during a collaborative group project. In writing the stories the way we did, we hoped to generate discussion of group inclusion at school, an acceptance–judgment theme that has been found to be particularly salient for elementary age students (Gottman & Parker, 1986).

As noted, stories involving the judgment–acceptance tension are ripe for discussing issues of inclusion and group acceptance. Stories involving diversity and difference, whether it is cultural or individual also fall into this theme. Through discussions of this nature, children have the opportunity to discern what's important in relating from what may be more superficial. At the same time, there is an acknowledgment of the need for standards. Clearly, we do have expectations of one another. The group can begin to clarify what standards are important to them and to make them explicit to each other. In this way, the RLC process provides an avenue for the classroom to evaluate and determine appropriate norms for inclusion within their classroom community.

TABLE 3.1

Judgment–Acceptance Hypothetical Stories

It was the start of another new school year. But this year Jamie was feeling anxious because her best friend was not going to be in her room anymore. In fact, her friend was not even coming back to the same school. Jamie was worried about who she was going to eat with and play with. It seemed like everything was going to be different this year, and she wasn't sure if she was going to like it.

Almost all the third-grade girls liked to play together on the playground. The group had known each other since kindergarten and they really got along well. Except there was one girl who didn't get included—Paula. Most of the others really didn't enjoy her very much. They usually avoided her at recess and lunch, made jokes behind her back, and even teased her right to her face. Nancy, one of the group members began to feel bad about what was happening to Paula. She thought about how she would feel if she were Paula. She wondered what she could do to change things.

Eric plays alone almost everyday at school. He would like to play more with the group—sometimes. One day Eric asks if he can play. The group says: "No, you can't play."

Bob is assigned to work on a project with Ted and Bill. Ted and Bill are good friends. They play together a lot at school. So when they start to work on the project, they talk mostly to each other. They don't listen to Bob or ask his opinion. When he tries to bring up an idea, they ignore or cut him off. One time when he says something they laugh at him and call him retard.

Lisa is a new girl in her class (third grade). She is quiet and a little shy. She's been just watching the others play at recess and really wanting to be part of the group, but she's not sure how they feel about her. And, she's not sure about how to get in with them.

Expressive–Protective

The dialectic of expressiveness and protectiveness refers to the tension between candor and restraint in communications with friends (Rawlins, 1992). Mutual expressiveness is often viewed as the hallmark of intimacy; however, unchecked openness can have negative consequences. One must be sensitive to how the other will react and sometimes exercise restraint in the information one shares. The maintenance of close relationships, then, requires careful consideration of the conditions under which candor is called for and those under which restraint may serve the relationship better (Rawlins, 1992). Rawlins argued that trust within a relationship is built upon careful negotiation of these two courses of action.

Middle childhood may be an important time for reflection on this tension. Children are becoming increasingly less tolerant of unchecked aggressiveness, temper outbursts, and bragging, and are beginning to be more sensitive to what actions hurt the feelings of another (Gottman & Parker, 1986; Sullivan, 1953). This evolving sensitivity seems characteristic of their developing ability to take the perspective of another. Children are beginning to better appreciate how certain uses of language can affect someone. They are interested and able to reflect on different ways the same message can be communicated with different effects. The goal of expressive–protective discussions, then, is to help children discern what is acceptable to them in peer and friendship communications and what is not. It is an opportunity for them to explore the emotional dimensions of interpersonal communication.

Discussions of expressive–protective stories can help children to explore communication between friends in greater detail. In these discussions, one can begin to hear some of the additional ingredients the children believe important in building strong relationships. Many of our expressive–protective hypothetical stories depicted situations where one friend needed to share feelings or concerns about the other friend that were difficult to express (see Table 3.2). Confronting a bossy friend or a friend who frequently lost his or her temper were typical examples of stories that related to the expressive–protective tension and that seemed pertinent to elementary students. Another situation involved the sharing of personal feelings with a friend.

The expressive–protective story context provides an excellent opportunity to explore the dimensions of constructive communication. How can feelings sometimes drive our communications with others? Under what relational circumstances can delicate feelings be expressed? How can feelings be expressed in healthy ways? The answers to these questions are complex and

TABLE 3.2

Expressive–Protective Hypothetical Stories

Sam and Pat are good friends. They play together at school and at home. They usually have a lot of fun, except for one problem. Sam can lose his temper pretty easily if something doesn't go his way. When he gets mad, the play just sort of stops or Pat lets Sam have his way. One time when it happened, Pat decided that he had to do something. He wanted Sam as a friend, but he really didn't like it when Sam lost his temper.

Jerry and Bobby have been pretty good friends at school. One day at recess they have a disagreement. When it's time to go inside they are still angry at each other. They never get a chance to talk any more that day. The next day at school, Bobby tells everyone that Jerry is mean and bossy and that they shouldn't play with Jerry.

Lee and Sam spend a lot of time together. They really enjoy sharing ideas. They like to talk about how different things work and stuff that is happening at school. They also like to talk about their favorite movies and books. But once in awhile Lee comes to school feeling down and depressed. Sometimes things happen at home, like his mom really getting mad at him and he feels upset. He would like to talk to Sam about these problems but he is not sure that he should.

Bob and Jeff are good friends. They play together a lot at school and at home. The only problem is that Bob loses his temper if he doesn't get his way when they play. One time when it happened, Jeff decided that he had to do something. He wanted Bob as a friend, but really didn't like it when he always lost his temper.

Lisa made friends with the girls and started to play with Jill and Patti almost every day at recess. She really liked them both a lot. There was only one problem though. Jill could sometimes be kind of bossy. She liked to tell Patti and Lisa what to do and how to play. One day, Patti and Lisa got really mad when Jill told them what to do. They really liked her but they didn't like her bossing them around. They really wanted to do something about it.

varied. Through the RLC stories, children can begin to articulate and examine their views.

Independence–Dependence

The independence–dependence tension references the problem of determining the degree of interdependence between individuals within a relationship. According to Rawlins (1992), the freedom to be independent and the freedom to be dependent reflect the voluntary nature of friendship. The freedom to be independent refers to a friend's ability to pursue his or her own interests without interference from the other. The freedom to be dependent refers to the privilege to call upon the other for support or assistance in times of need. The nature of this balance is continually negotiated and defined between friends through their interactions and communications. It would seem that a balance is needed to maintain a healthy bond within the friendship.

Rawlins (1992) speculated that the independence–dependence distinction would gradually acquire meaning for children. Young children's friendships have been characterized as fleeting, and thus, strongly independent (Corsaro, 1985; Gottman & Parker, 1986; Selman, 1980). Older children, however, begin to comprehend the voluntary nature of friendship and attempt to maintain more dependent and mutual relationships (Selman, 1980; Selman & Schultz, 1990). Feelings of possessiveness and jealously can emerge regarding a friend's autonomous choices. A salient context for this tension is when friends grow apart. One friend may experience this as particularly painful, feeling rejected and lonely. Children need opportunities to explore their views and feelings around individual growth and change and the effects of that on their relationships with others. The goal of independence–dependence discussions, then, is to explore the nature of interdependency in the peer relationships within the classroom and how natural changes may shift the balance in our relationships. These discussions can help children to discern the boundaries of self and other in patterns of relating.

In our work with children, we have represented this dilemma through a variety of stories (see Table 3.3). Several of these stories depict threesomes having difficulty coordinating their play. In our experience, this was a somewhat frequent occurrence among the second and third graders. In other instances, a twosome is struggling to organize their play in the context of a larger group or two friends have grown apart. In all of them, we attempted to depict the characters struggling to negotiate a discrepancy between their own desires, needs, and beliefs and those of significant others.

TABLE 3.3

Independence–Dependence Hypothetical Stories

Once there were three really good friends named Jill, Molly, and El-len. They had been friends for quite a few years. This year Ellen sud-denly started to draw away from Jill and Molly and play with other people. Sometimes Ellen even was mean to Jill and Molly making them feel that they had done something to hurt her. Jill and Molly felt really confused. They didn't understand why Ellen was moving away from them and why she was mean to them sometimes. They didn't want to lose her friendship, but they didn't know what to do.

Terry, Lee, and Francis were good friends. They play together a lot at school and at home after school. The only problem sometimes is that they have a hard time deciding what to play. Like one day, Lee wanted to play kickball outside and Francis wanted to play a computer game. Terry wasn't sure what she wanted to do, but then decided she wanted to play on the computer. Lee got upset and said, "That's not fair, if you guys don't play ball, I'm going home." Then Terry and Fran-cis felt upset and weren't sure what to do.

Jake and Alec are really good friends. They usually eat lunch together and play on the jungle gym at recess. Sometimes other kids join them, but Jake really doesn't like that. He would rather play with Alec by himself. When Alec is not in school, Jake is kind of lost. He wan-ders by himself at lunch break. But when Jake is out, Alec usually joins another group to play. One time after Jake had been out sick for several days, Alec wanted Jake to join him in playing with the group he had been playing with while Jake was out. Jake was upset. He thought that Alec should just play with him because they were best friends.

Terry and Pat have a lot of fun together at school. Sometimes Pat can get carried away though and do some crazy things. He does things that can get them into trouble. Terry isn't sure what to do. He wants to play with Pat but he doesn't want to get into trouble.

Jill and Patti were really good friends. They lived on the same block and played with their Barbie® dolls together almost every Saturday. Lisa moved into the neighborhood and started to play with Jill and Patti. She liked to play computer games and got the girls to play that once in a while. Jill really didn't like to play on the computer much, but Patti sometimes liked to do that. When Lisa suggested it, Jill tried to get Patti to say no and play with her instead. Patti felt torn. She didnt want to hurt Jill, but she sometimes wanted to play something different with someone else.

The independence–dependence stories provide an opportunity to explore the degree of separation between individuals in a relationship. Clearly there are different patterns in this regard. We have observed children articulate patterns that may signal overly dependent relating and those that signal overly independent relating. It is helpful for them to begin to discern these patterns of interaction and to reflect upon what is comfortable for them. Stories involving this tension have resonated with many children who are experiencing the push and pull of different relationships in the classroom. As they struggle to determine their allegiance to one individual–group or another, it is important for them to have the opportunity to reflect on this tension.

Instrumentality–Affection

The dialectic of instrumentality–affection within friendship refers to the tension between caring for the friend as an end in itself and caring for the friend as a means to an end (Rawlins, 1992). All of our relationships involve both of these poles to some extent. Surely we do choose friends for the ways in which they elaborate our lives. Overly utilitarian relationships, however, can result in feelings of hurt and betrayal. These stories provide children with an opportunity to reflect on what this means to them.

In our work with younger elementary age students, we have discussed stories associated with instrumentality and affection somewhat less frequently than the other four tensions. In our observations of the children's own conflicts, this tension seemed less salient. Rawlins (1992) suggested that minimal distinctions may exist between affection and instrumentality in the relationships of children. Children frequently consider someone a friend because the person's toys or attributes are pleasing to him or her (Damon, 1977; Selman, 1980). As children approach adolescence, however, the tension may become more meaningful.

Our stories for the instrumentality–affection tension depicted interactions in which one child or a group of children were being taken advantage of by a peer. In one case, the child realizes there is a problem when his computer game breaks and the friend no longer wants to play with him. In another scenario, two boys enjoy the help of a third in the classroom, but never think to ask this boy to join them on the playground (see Table 3.4).

Stories depicting the instrumentality–affection tension offer an opportunity to focus on variations in the limits of different relationships. Sometimes we have relationships for specific purposes or related to specific contexts (e.g., friends we have only at

TABLE 3.4
Instrumentality–Affection Hypothetical Stories

Alex and Chris often like to play computer games together after school at Chris' house. One day at lunch, Chris mentioned to Alex that his game was broken and that they couldn't get it fixed for awhile. The next day when Chris asked Alex to come over, Alex hesitated. And then Alex said that he wasn't going to come because he wanted to play computer games so he was going to see if he could go to Marty's house to play. Chris felt upset and confused. He wanted to play with Alex, but wasn't sure what to do.

Chris is really good at reading and figuring out math problems. Pat and Aaron, some of his classmates, like to work with him during group work. They usually have a pretty good time in class, but when recess comes, Pat and Aaron just run out the door and leave Chris behind. Chris would like to play with them at recess too, but he's not sure that they really want to play with him at recess. He's not sure what to do.

Frank and Paul liked to work together in class. Frank was a good reader. He helped Paul understand words and ideas that were difficult in reading. Paul was good in math. He knew all his facts really well and liked to think about the story problems. He usually helped Frank with these. So they shared the things they were really good at with each other. One day Bill was having trouble with math work. He came to Paul for help and got a lot of help. Bill started coming back everyday, trying to be friendly but always asking for help. Paul started to get tired of it. Helping Bill didn't feel the same as helping Frank, but Paul wasn't sure what to do.

Betty and Sue are good friends at school. One day Betty promised to help Sue sell cookies at the bake sale after school. Tammy ran into Betty when she was on her way and talked her into going to play volleyball in the gym instead. When Sue saw Betty the next day, she asked her what happened. Beth lied and said her mom called and she had to go home. Just then Tammy walked by and said, "Wasn't volleyball fun yesterday after school? Want to do it again?" Betty felt really embarrassed and awkward. Sue got really mad.

summer camps; swimteam friends). Other times we have relationships that cut across a variety of contexts. The latter seem to epitomize our true or best friends. It's important for children to discern patterns of relating in these various relationships in their lives and to understand how the variety of relationships may be important to them.

Summary

We have spent considerable time in this chapter discussing the dialectic tension framework (Rawlins, 1992) and its relationship to story development in order to provide teachers with a deeper understanding of this critical aspect of the RLC. In our work with children, we have been surprised and impressed by the power of the dialectic tensions in providing a framework for students to explore relational issues in their discussion. They have engaged in powerful discussions. For this reason, the use of the dialectic tensions to develop stories and frame the discussions is essential to the RLC. Teachers interested in implementing the RLC should take the time to reflect on the tensions and understand their dialectic nature, as knowledge of this is central to successful implementation. In the following section of this chapter, we review and explore the discussion process in which the tensions are utilized.

REFLECTING ON RLC DISCUSSIONS

In this half of the chapter, we focus on the process of the RLC discussions. We begin by reviewing the basic problem-solving questioning process and provide standards for assessing the overall quality of the discussion. Second, we focus in on the nature of the explanations children tend to provide, and provide a developmental framework to assess the complexity of their explanations. Finally, we turn to the various ways the teacher may prompt the children during the discussion and how these may relate to the children's explanations and the overall quality of the discussion.

The Basic Discussion

Recall that the basic RLC discussions are based upon a problem-solving model. The process begins by the teacher reading a brief story like those previously described to the class. The teacher then initiates the discussion by asking the class: **What is the problem in the story?** With this question, the teacher is eliciting the essential facts of the story and what the problem is in very simple terms. For example, in our judgment–acceptance story about Eric, the problem definition is simply that Eric wants to play and the group says no.

Once the literal facts and problem definition are satisfactorily achieved, the teacher moves on to the second major question: **Why do things like this happen?** In response to this question, children provide possible explanations for the dilemma in the story. All explanations are accepted without evaluation. This is akin to a brainstorming session. The aim is to elicit a variety of viewpoints. This segment of the discussion calls for inferential comprehension of the story. Children draw upon their world knowledge to make reasonable guesses about the situation while making connections to situations like this that they have encountered and principles of interaction that they may have implicitly learned. With respect to our example story about Eric, the children might talk about the protagonist as being different or having done something to offend the group in the past. Children love this segment of the discussion and often have difficulty moving on. They truly enjoy exercising their powers of imagination about the potential motives and views of others. Periodically, however, some children will be in a hurry to offer solutions in the form of action choices for the characters. Teachers must be alert to this and help the children to differentiate the phases of the discussion. It is important that they all come to understand where they are in the discussion process and the kinds of information that are being shared.

After the potential explanations have been exhausted, teachers pose the final question: **What are some choices?** Here children offer solutions for the dilemma under discussion in terms of choices that the characters can make. Choices are also elicited in brainstorming fashion with no evaluation of potential ideas. Table 3.5 summarizes the basic process. Note that we have highlighted the why question. As we indicated in chapter 2, this is the heart of the RLC process. We elaborate upon the possible types of explanations that children may provide in Table

TABLE 3.5
The Basic Discussion Process

Teacher	Children
What is the problem?	Literal facts from the story
	Literal problem definition
Why do things like this happen?	Inferential thinking
	Explanations for relational conflicts
What are some choices?	Action choices for characters
	Problem resolution

3.5 as well as teacher prompts that facilitate this aspect of the discussion process.

As the discussion moves along, teachers record all the children's responses on a large chart paper (See Table 2.1 for sample recording notes). In this way, the children can remember and reflect on what has been said. It helps all to keep track of the discussion and to make their own contributions as it moves along. The teachers also have a brief record of what has been said. In this way, they can keep track of the themes discussed and the views that have been shared. We have found that it is important to record the children's own language as much as possible, rather than to paraphrase it. They often have unique and powerful phrases to explain their experiences that capture the feelings of other children well. In this way, the group can achieve one of the goals of the RLC—evolving a shared language for the issues that are important to them.

Elements of a Good Discussion

A key aspect of the RLC is a rich discussion utilizing the problem-solving questions. A good discussion is not necessarily an automatic for all children in all classrooms. Therefore in this section, we give guidance for promoting and assessing a good classroom discussion. In planning for and reflecting on RLC discussions, it's important to consider the experiences the children have had with such discussions. Is this a regular feature of your curriculum or is this something new? What skills and expectations do the children have in this regard? What are your expectations and skills? Classrooms where group dialogue has not been prevalent may need more support and more time in working toward quality discussions. They do not happen automatically. The children may need to be prompted to listen and respond to each other if this has not been emphasized before. It is important to have reasonable expectations based upon the history of discussions the group has had.

In Table 3.6, we provide a framework to help teachers judge and guide the quality of the discussion. Overall, the standards in this framework reflect a belief in the importance of children talking to each other rather than simply responding to the teacher. It is important to the goals of the curriculum that children listen and respond to each other; that they build on each other's ideas; and that they show an interest in what others are saying by questioning them. We want to see a balance of teacher and child talk, and preferably more child than teacher talk. Ta-

TABLE 3.6
Quality Discussion Rubric

Quality	Not Yet Observed	Emerging	Frequently Evident	Ongoing
Children make comments that connect to other children				
Children question each other				
Children listen to each other				
Children respond to each other				
Children stay on topic and develop a shared idea				
Goals of discussion are clear to all				

ble 3.6 contains the specific features we are looking for in regard to a quality discussion. For groups that may have had little opportunity to discuss as a whole class, these standards may take time and practice to emerge. The essential purpose of these discussions is for children to take ownership of the ideas and the issues. It is important for them to articulate their feelings and views, and to listen and reflect on the views of others. This cannot happen in an authentic way if the teacher dominates the talk.

We encourage teachers to audiotape and review the RLC discussions as they are beginning this work. In this way, they may review and assess a discussion according to the different dimensions of the discussion. If audiotaping isn't feasible, a quick written reflection following the discussion may still be useful in determining whether a group is working toward the goals of the RLC. The rubric illustrated in Table 3.6 is intended as a written reflection tool to review the quality of the discussion as a whole. The categories for assessing the discussion reflect a developmental perspective. A complete rubric that may be copied for teacher use is provided in Appendix B.

Anticipating Child Explanations

When facilitating the children's discussions of why a conflict may be happening, it is important to have a scheme or framework for organizing what they say. Indeed, the children's understanding of relationships can be discerned through their explanation of the conflict. The more general RLC goal of elaborating the children's understanding of their relationships can be achieved by paying attention to and encouraging more complex explanations.

After examining transcripts from several years of RLC discussions, we derived a category scheme for describing the different explanation types that children tend to provide for the interpersonal conflicts (Salmon & Freedman, 2000). This category scheme can be useful in discerning children's understanding as well as facilitating more complex ways of knowing. Table 3.7 contains a description and examples of each of the explanation types we have found in our data.

TABLE 3.7
Quality of Child Explanations

No Explanation	Simply stating that such events just happen ("people are just that way").
Character Interpretations	References to character thoughts, feelings, traits, and mental states ("Alex is greedy"; "Alex doesn't want to go to Chris' because his computer is broken.").
Circumstances	References to events or people outside of the main characters' relationship ("Alex doesn't have a computer"; "Alex may have had a date already to play computers.").
Character Differences	References to differences in opinion, views, and personality of characters ("Alex is a computer freak, Chris is not"; "They want different things.").
Character Interactions	References to history of actions and reactions ("Alex might have hogged the computer and Alex didn't want to hurt her feelings, so she's secretly glad its broken.").
Relationship	References to qualities of the relationship as a whole ("When they played they had fun, but without the computer they weren't such good friends"; "They are computer friends only.").
Metaphors or Personal Stories	References that provide connections to other knowledge or experience by going beyond the given story to metaphors or personal stories related to the theme ("Their friendship is like a rubberband"; "They are like sisters.").

The explanation categories in Table 3.7 are roughly hierarchical with each successive category becoming broader and implicitly capturing information referenced in explanations of prior categories. That is, as you move up the hierarchy, more features are implicitly referenced within the episode that is being discussed. In this regard, the explanation types reflect different degrees of complexity. At the lowest level, children offer essentially no explanation for the event. These usually involve reflections such as it just happens. At the next level, character interpretations, the children focus on one of the people in the story, referencing their feelings, beliefs, behavior, or character traits. Explanations referring to circumstances implicitly acknowledge an interpretation of the character but call attention to circumstances that may play a role. In explanations involving character differences, the children need to focus on both characters at once, their personality or points of view. Explanations involving character interactions tend to describe a series of actions and reactions. In this regard, the children view an episode unfolding over time. Relationship explanations implicitly acknowledge information about the characters and their interactions referring to these as an integrated whole. In the highest explanation type, children provide a personal story or a metaphor that captures the essential tension in the dilemma.

This scheme of explanation types roughly parallels cognitive developmental research on children's development of perspective-taking abilities (Selman, 1980; Selman & Schultz, 1990; Selman, Watts, & Schultz, 1997). The higher-level explanations such as character interactions or relationship explanations suggest that a child sees more within the event than simple character interpretations. The more complex the explanation within our scheme, the more information they are taking into account in explaining the problem. Teachers, then, can think of these categories of explanations as targets in the discussion, and use this framework to encourage and challenge more complex thinking from their students. An easy way to discern the quality of the explanations is to review the children's responses to why the problem may be happening that is recorded on the large chart paper during discussions. Teachers may wish to retype these and code the child responses to why the problem is occurring. In this way, they have a record of the children's explanations and how they may grow through the year.

We provide additional examples of these explanation types in the context of the following judgment–acceptance tension. Recall that the implicit goal of discussions involving this tension is to surface and examine one's standards for accepting and judging others. As children move from narrow character interpretations to more sophisticated explanations, they also construct more contextual and relational criteria for judging or accepting others.

The following excerpt provides an example explanation involving a **character interpretation**.

Children: He's nerdy.

Teacher: So, wait, hold on, Jay, say what you mean.

Jay: Couldn't act like cool, he's not cool.

Teacher: So are you talking about his personality?

Jay: Yeah.

In this example, the boys focus on personality characteristics that may cause the character to not be accepted by the group. In other examples of character interpretations, the children call attention to physical characteristics that may be considered when individuals are not included. The following is another example of the same explanation type focusing on valued skills.

Mark: He doesn't know how to play.

Teacher: So it might happen because—

Mark: He doesn't know how to play, so they don't want to waste their time teaching him.

The following is another version of a character lacking skills, but one that moves toward a more contextual explanation.

Helen: She just doesn't know how to ask them.

Teacher: Doesn't know how to ask them.

Jane: She, it is a different, different than her school ... and she doesn't know how to make friends.

Teacher: So it could be a new school and

Jane: She doesn't know how to make a friend.

Eve: Yea. yea.

As this discussion progressed, the children elaborated on why the character may not know how to ask to play. Although still largely focusing on a character in their interpretation, they bring in an explanation involving the **circumstances** of the school culture. Their explanation moved beyond a single focus on the individual to include the context and the history of the character's experience. In the next example, the children again bring in the history of the characters to help explain their behavior.

Tera:	Maybe she had a bad day and her, and she made a mistake and she had a bad day and said something wrong.
Teacher:	Is this connected to why she got in a fight?
Tera:	No. She said something wrong, to someone who wasn't her friend and then they tattled all over the place to all her friends and then and they sort of exaggerated it so that was something mean and then they didn't want to play with her.

In this example, Tera describes a history of interactions between the characters that help to explain the group's exclusion of the protagonist. This type of explanation focusing on **character interactions** moves beyond simple character trait explanations to consider action and interaction over time. This latter explanation offers more than one perspective and suggests the complexity that different perspectives can offer. Moreover, one can also see that the more contextual explanations lend themselves to more constructive action choices. For example, when someone is considered less experienced because of their background of experience or when a prior transgression has occurred, the choices for resolution are more readily apparent than when a problem has occurred simply because a character is considered a nerd.

The following dialogue excerpt is taken from another discussion involving the judgment–acceptance tension. The explanations generated by the students' focus on the **relationship**.

Teacher:	Why does a problem like this happen?
Mark:	They are not good friends. They are enemies.
Teacher:	What have you guys observed about enemies? Why do people become enemies?

Larry:	Well I had some friends, and there was this kid named Stu and they were once friends. But then he told a lie about his neighbors so they didn't like each other at all and now they get really really mad at each other.
Teacher:	So people lie to each other and they become enemies.
Paul:	Their friendship is an illusion.
Teacher:	Their friendship is an illusion. What do you mean by that?
Paul:	Well I mean, at first they were friends for about I don't know a few months, and then they got into this fight and then they go into another one, so they don't really have a friendship between all this. There is nothing to really, that really got them into knowing each other.

In this discussion, the children are making important connections around their concepts of friends and enemies. In the first explanation, Mark remarks on the relationship, while Larry shares a **personal story** involving children who were once friends and lost their friendship due to lies. Paul seems to recast Larry's personal story in terms of a **metaphor**, "the friendship is really an illusion." He goes on to explain this as something they thought they had, but perhaps they never really did. Again, one can see the greater complexity in a relational explanation. The children are focusing on the interactions between characters and the characters' thinking about those interactions. The use of metaphor and personal story facilitate these kinds of communications and can be extremely powerful in making the issues and concepts come alive.

The hierarchy of explanation types can be a helpful guide in gauging children thinking about friendship and relational conflict. Most often, the children readily provide character interpretations in their explanations. As these are laid on the table, they may gradually offer more dynamic explanations that involve circumstances, interactional history, and relational accounts. One can see in the previous examples that the more contextual explanations are more useful than those focused only on an individual. They provide more information, take more perspectives into account, and suggest more constructive action choices. Teacher prompts can often make a difference in the occurrence of more complex explanations. In the next section, we introduce a category scheme for reflecting on teacher questions.

Reflecting on Teacher Prompts

How can teachers think about the quality of their own talk in a discussion? How can they use this knowledge to help children to achieve more complex explanations of conflict and greater quality discussions? The teacher's role in fostering children's explanations is extremely important. Two important principles stand out in regard to this. First, **honoring and encouraging the children's own language** is central to this role. Second, **asking effective questions at the right time** can be of equal importance. In working with teachers to implement the RLC, we have developed a category scheme for the kinds of prompts that teachers use during the discussion (Salmon & Freedman, 1999). This scheme can be helpful in reflecting upon and critiquing your own role in the discussion process. Table 3.8 lists the key prompts teachers use during RLC discussions.

This simple scheme ranges from teacher prompts that focus mainly on managing the students' behavior to prompts that seek to explore relational concepts. Similar to the categories for the children's explanations, these prompts reflect a gradual shift in complexity. In this scheme, they shift from a focus on behavior to a focus on concepts. Process prompts focus the children's attention on the basic RLC questions. Restatement prompts simply reflect what the children have said to keep the discussion moving or to clarify their comments. Elaboration prompts attempt to build on what a child has said by encouraging a more expansive response. Concept prompts attempt to move the children's thinking beyond the story under discussion to a bigger relational idea that cuts across relational contexts.

The most common type of prompt is the management and the restatement prompts. One can see several examples of these in the excerpts of dialogue we previously provided. Elaboration

TABLE 3.8

Teacher Prompts

Management Prompts	Prompts that focus on classroom management and calling on students.
Process Prompts	Prompts the students about the process: What is the problem?, Why do things like this happen?, and What are some choices?
Restating Student's Ideas Prompts	Prompts that restate the students' ideas and clarifies their comments.
Elaboration Prompts	Prompts that specifically pursue ideas stated by the children.
Concept Prompts	Prompts that explore big ideas, refer to the dialectic tensions, or both. Prompts that extend the students' thinking beyond the story.

prompts and conceptual prompts tend to be more infrequent, but are more critical to the quality of the overall discussion and the complexity of the explanations that the children explore. We illustrate the occurrence of these various prompts in the following excerpts. These excerpts come from a discussion of the expressive–protective story in which two friends have an argument at school. As a result of the argument, one friend tells negative stories about the other friend.

> Teacher: Okay. Okay, I think we've got everything up there for our problem. Sue was telling everybody not to play with Lisa. Sue and Lisa are being mean to each other and they're not seeing each other and they're having an argument. Why do you think this is possibly happening? **[Restatement; Process Prompt]**
>
> Lynn: Well, maybe because they were like enemies. Before they didn't go together but then they became friends, but they were more like bad friends.

Teacher: So their friendship wasn't real good? **[Restatement]**

Lynn: Yea.

Teacher: Okay, why else could things like this happen? **[Process Prompt]**

Denny: Well like before they were nice and then they get mean because her best friend did something mean like saying something mean about her.

Teacher: So you're saying that Sue in our story was being mean because Lisa was being mean to her? So maybe Lisa was the one that was mean and Sue was just doing something back? That kind of thing? **[Elaboration Prompt]**

Denny: Yea, to get someone back.

In this excerpt, the group is beginning the discussion of why things like this happen. The teacher begins this transition by restating in summary form the problem definition that the children have generated. She finishes with the process prompt of why is this happening. We see two different explanations offered here. The first is that the girls never had a very strong friendship in the first place. The second seems to elaborate on this notion more concretely by describing their interactions in terms of one girl getting back at the other for past transgressions. After the first explanation, the teacher restates the first explanation and then elicits the second explanation. After the second explanation is offered, the teacher restates the child's response again but seems to go a little farther this time clarifying and perhaps elaborating a bit on what the child said. This is sometimes important to do, so that everyone can check his or her understanding of what was said. Frequently, children struggle to put their ideas into words, and they need modeling and support from the teacher in organizing their response.

Teacher: Okay. Why else would somebody say mean things about somebody else. Why would you do that? Tina? **[Process Prompt]**

Tina: Because Lisa told another one of their good
            friends one of the secrets that Sue told her.

Teacher: Okay, so maybe Lisa told somebody a secret
            that she wasn't supposed to, one of Sue's se-
            crets. How would that make someone feel?
            [Elaboration Prompt]

Allen: Very mad because you thought you could trust
            them.

Teacher: So Lisa told a secret of Sue's and that made her
            feel mad ... kind of broke her trust. **[Restate-
            ment Prompt]**

In this second excerpt, we see a continuation of the discussion
of why this conflict might have occurred. Another explanation
focusing on the characters' interactions is offered. The teacher
moves from the process prompt to an elaborative prompt and
concludes this interaction with a restatement. Shortly following
this exchange, the teacher redirects the discussion toward the
expressive–protective tension in the story.

Teacher: Can I ask you guys a question? Do you ever find
            it hard to tell a friend something you don't like
            that they are doing? **[Conceptual Prompt]**

Leah: Yeah.

Teacher: Tell me about it. **[Elaboration Prompt]**

Leah: It's like, it's like you want to tell them but they
            might, you think like they won't listen to you.

Teacher: So you are afraid that they won't listen to you.
            What else makes it hard? **[Restatement; Elabo-
            ration Prompt]**

Mark: It's hard because he thinks that he'll get mad
            and he won't want to see him any more.

Teacher: Okay, I'm going to write these things down. So
            one was afraid that the friend won't listen. And
            the other was afraid that they'll get mad. **[Re-
            statement]**

In this segment, the teacher is encouraging the children to explore what makes it difficult to express difficult feelings to others. Here the children offer two explanations that reflect potential feelings the other may have and responses they may take. Slightly later in the discussion, the teacher offers another conceptual prompt.

Teacher:	Can I ask you another question related to this idea? If you never tell them, the thing that bothers you, if you just ignore it, what do you think happens to the friendship? **[Conceptual Prompt]**
Mike:	They might get mad at each other and never talk to each other again.
Teacher:	Yeah, good point. **[Management Prompt]**
Tina:	You know, after awhile it will really bug you and you will think but I don't really like her, well I don't have anything in common with her anymore.
Teacher:	So it kind of builds up until it really bugs you? **[Restatement]**

Here again the teacher pursues the expressive–protective tension in the story by exploring the consequences of an overly protective stance. The children offer explanations that suggest that they are well aware of the consequences of not talking about problems.

Conceptual prompts typically move the children somewhat away from the specifics of the story to get them thinking about the deeper issue. These prompts can often result in personal stories and other connections that children are making. One or two of these per discussion are usually sufficient. Too many and the discussion may become too teacher directed. Too few conceptual prompts and the discussion may remain on a simplistic level. Conceptual prompts ought to help the children become aware of the contradictions involved in relating. In the case of the previous example, the children were focusing during much of the discussion on how saying mean things can spoil a friend-

ship. The conceptual prompts were designed to get them thinking about the necessity to sometimes say things that may be
difficult and on the surface appear mean. We do sometimes need
to tell friends things that they don't want to hear. RLC discussions that are working well ought to be surfacing these kinds of
contradictions and allowing children to explore their meaning.
The following is another example from an judgment–acceptance
discussion.

> Teacher: Is there, do you think that there is ever a time
> and a place to judge your friends? And what
> would that be like?
>
> Jan: You play with them a long time and you know
> them really well, and they are like your best
> friend. Then you can judge and know for your-
> self that they are really nice and they are always
> going to be your friend.

Here the teacher tries to draw the children's attention to the
contradiction in the acceptance–judgment tension. In the
brief stories depicting exclusionary interactions, it is easy for
the children to adopt a simple view that exclusion is always
bad. However, the issue is typically more complex and conceptual prompts, such as this one, are often needed to focus the
children's attention on both sides of the judgment–acceptance
tension.

Experience with the RLC discussions is important for teachers to discern opportunities to interject conceptual prompts. In
addition, knowing the needs of one's students is also a source of
information in formulating the best prompts to stimulate more
conceptually challenging discussions. We provide additional examples of potentially useful conceptual prompts for each relational tension in Appendix B.

Summary

In this chapter, we reviewed and illustrated the basic RLC discussion process. One of the most important elements is the
story that is used to generate discussion. We provided general

guidelines for creating these stories as well as examples of several that we have used for children in second through fourth grade. The four dialectic tensions of judgment–acceptance, expressiveness–protectiveness, independence–dependence, and instrumentality–affection provide a framework for the types of conflict in the stories.

The discussion process is organized around a problem-solving model. We reviewed these questions as well as the kinds of child and teacher talk that may emerge around them. We suggested frameworks for observing the nature of the children's explanations and for reflecting on the teacher–leader's prompts. Appendix B contains tools and other quick reference supplemental materials for planning stories and assessing the discussions.

4

Role Playing
in the Relational
Literacy Curriculum

Christopher J. Fogartaigh
National-Louis University

"You can't really say something mean in a nice way ..."

INTRODUCTION

Once children have been introduced to the relationship stories and have explored them through discussion, it is time to put their emerging constructs into action. In this chapter, we will discuss how teachers can successfully lead role play sessions so that students can strengthen their interpersonal knowledge and continue to direct the curriculum based on their own needs and developing perspectives.

First, we begin by providing some of the background on the efficacy of role playing in educational contexts and the relationship between basic role play goals and the goals of the RLC. Then, we turn to a developmental framework for thinking about a role play progression throughout the school year. Within this framework, we outline three distinct phases a teacher can follow in order to maximize the learning experience through a steady, slow increase of challenges for the students to tackle. As well, this framework provides a way for teachers to examine the progress of individual students. Finally, we explore some further considerations for teachers to be aware of in order to make the most of the role play sessions.

PURPOSES OF THE RLC ROLE PLAY

Role playing as an action method was first developed by Moreno (1953) as the fundamental process of psychodrama and sociodrama, of which he wrote that "the concept underlying this approach is the recognition that man is a role player, that every individual is characterized by a certain range of roles which dominate his behavior ... (p. 60). As a means of interpersonal, group, and educational growth, role playing has since become an integral part of various other disciplines such as creative drama, drama therapy, and educational drama. Moreno defined the term as "playing a role, by choice, in a chosen setting for the purpose of exploring, experimenting, developing, and training" (Moreno, 1953, p. 279). We have concentrated on the spirit of this definition, though there are many others, because it seems to best focus on goals consistent with those of the RLC.

Recapitulating briefly, the RLC goals focus upon the following:

- Elaborating and refining understandings of friendship and other relationships.
- Developing a language with which to share and clarify social experiences.
- Providing a process through which group norms can be explored, articulated, and critiqued.
- Fostering independent social problem strategies.

The dramatic activities within the RLC further elaborate these goals by connecting with the educational frameworks of perspectival learning, spontaneity, and inventiveness, and knowing by doing in the creation of real contexts.

The role play process, and perhaps all dramatic activity, is chiefly concerned with broadening one' s perspective through exploring and acknowledging the many points of view an individual may bring to a situation. This is accomplished both through engaging in role play as well as observing others, especially peers, role play (Rogoff, 1990). Play offers an opportunity to do this in a manner that cannot be attained through conversation alone. It brings the metaphorical aspects of language to life and allows for a deeper exploration of ideas by fostering a more personal and immediate interaction with the perspectives of oneself and of others. It is the difference, for example, between talking about teaching a class and actually teaching a class. It is the difference between talking about doing something and actually doing that something. Role playing lets us move beyond talking about perspectives by allowing us to interact with those perspectives as they unfold in the moment of their genesis.

Spontaneity and inventiveness, as well, are particularly helpful in the social problem-solving process (Courtney, 1990). These qualities, infused into the role play experience, help individuals search for meaning and novel solutions through perpetually allowing students to experiment with the efficacy of their thoughts and feelings in a social context. According to Moreno, once people have formed adequate responses to a situation they tend to fall back on these responses because they are already established in one's role repertoire and, thus, are easier to perform because they take less consideration and effort. Through improvisation, students are discouraged from relying on pre-existing methods of action and thought. Instead, they must invent or intuit new ways of thinking and behaving based solely on the situation in which they find themselves. As Cantor and Kihlstrom (1987) wrote, "most life tasks are worked on in the course of social interactions in which the situation itself is constantly changing shape ... (and) problem-solving strategies unfold in fits and starts, often interrupted by the necessity to attend to new problems as they arise" (p. 188). Hence, role playing in the RLC provides a structured process in which students can explore and experiment with novel strategies for negotiating their social world.

Finally, the role play allows students to know by doing. During discussion sessions in the RLC we ask students to talk about what they think, how they feel, and what they'd do; during the role play sessions we ask them to live it, to show us, to experience it. Role playing allows the students to get closer to more realistic situations by enabling them to perform "as if" (Blatner, 1988; Courtney, 1990). In this simulated context, students can draw from and project onto the actual conditions of their social lives; thereby, making a stronger connection between what is abstract or implicit and what is concrete or explicit.

RLC ROLE PLAY GOALS

The general goals of role playing within the RLC are threefold:

• To allow students the opportunity to build upon the relational constructs that have been emerging through discussion sessions by acting them out.

• To help students get a better understanding of how classmates think about and portray their own thinking about relationships.

• To provide the teacher with more information on student development as well as offering another forum for further discussion.

The first goal, that of allowing students to put their ideas and perspectives into action, has to it many components. In one sense, it simply involves providing students with the opportunity to explore the natural outcome of their work. Since the curriculum is concerned with social relationships, it is only fitting that students display their work, so to speak, in a pointedly social context. As with most any subject, children are exposed to concepts, think about them, share their thoughts with others, and then display the results of their efforts. Thus, role playing offers an alternative method for students to display their perceptions of the relationship process. We have, in fact, come to find, consistent with Gardner's theories (1983), that many students who may not be verbally reflective or sufficiently engaged in classroom discourse can illustrate their social and interpersonal intelligence remarkably well through action.

Through role playing, students also have the opportunity to further gauge their own thinking in a context that supports immediate personal reflection, allowing them to "examine a situation and take part in a sequence of events, thereby gaining an understanding of the reality they may face outside the classroom" (Chiodo & Klausmeier, 1984, p. 122). When students role play in the RLC, they are testing out their ideas about how and why relationship problems exist in a way they cannot during discussion alone. Through enacting their understandings, they may ask themselves "Does this feel right to me?" "Is this really how I would react?" It gets the students to assess the authenticity of their relational constructs and, by doing so, elevates the learning experience.

The second goal, that of allowing students the opportunity to witness how their classmates portray similar relationship episodes, is essentially a matter of supporting the learning that has taken place during class discussions. Observing how peers role play provides another educational forum from which students can internalize new ideas and perspectives, as well as gain new insights about other students. It is a step beyond listening to their classmates and teacher. Here, they watch how others enact their ideas and again, as members of the audience, they can gauge the authenticity of the performance and its relevancy to their own ways of understanding.

The third goal of the role play sessions involves both the students and the teacher. For the students, it is another opportunity to talk about relationship issues. Being either a participant or an observer, the children now have new information and a new context. Whereas in discussions centered on the how and why questions of relationships the students were dealing chiefly with abstract ideas, in the role play those ideas have been given life. They can now address characters that represent what was once only an idea and, they can now interact with that idea on a whole different level. For the teacher, the role play and the discussions focused around the role play afford a new perspective in which to assess student development through the curriculum, learn more about the children's social worlds, and connect with them on a more personal level.

A DEVELOPMENTAL FRAMEWORK
FOR CONCEPTUALIZING THE ROLE PLAY

The framework for implementing role playing with the RLC is based upon the theoretical work of Moreno's (1953) conceptions of role, work within educational drama and drama therapy, and the observations we have made while conducting the RLC over the past seven years. We have found, consistent with Moreno's role theory (1953), three basic types of role play styles that a teacher can expect to find. In addition to categorizing how individual students will approach the role play activity, these three styles, which can roughly be viewed as points along a developmental continuum, also reflect a process of the role play development throughout the curriculum that teachers may follow in order to maximize the learning experience. These three styles, in Moreno's terms, are Role Taking, Role Playing, and Role Creating.

Phase 1: Role Taking–Stereotyping Range

Role taking is "the taking of a finished, fully established role which does not permit the individual any variation, any degree of freedom ... it is an attitude already frozen in the behavior of a person" (Moreno, 1953, p. 48). One could think of this in terms of stereotypical behavior. As members of a group or culture, most of us have shared assumptions about how certain roles are performed and maintained. We might all, for example, have similar conceptions of how a mother, a father, a policeman, or a teacher perform their general roles. Though we know that there are many individual differences people have while carrying out roles, we may still have a shared notion of what these roles look like. We may, for instance, tend to define the role of an elementary teacher with descriptions such as female, intelligent, caring, and nurturing. Of course, these descriptors do not accurately portray all elementary school teachers, but within a given culture these words might come to mind for a great deal of the population. One could also conceive of role taking as synonymous with an actor reading from a script. All the lines have been written, with indication as to what thoughts and feelings are to arise, as well, perhaps when to stand, sit, cross the stage, and exit and enter the scene. There is little room for individual variation.

Moreno's role taking has a correlation in the fields of educational drama and drama therapy, defined by Sandberg (1981) as the stereotyping range. Someone who is operating in this range is rigid in their performance, lacking the necessary creative resources to inhabit and explore a character. As well, the stereotyping range refers to individuals who have difficulty reflecting on their role play experience.

Role plays in educational drama, drama therapy, and our own observations with the RLC, have shown that when individuals are first introduced to this sort of activity they tend to be anxious, nervous, and ill-prepared. Even those students who are at ease performing in front of others tend to focus more on the attention they receive just being in the spotlight, rather than at the work at hand. For this reason, it is helpful to begin role plays with a lot of structure for the purpose of minimizing children's inhibitions (Johnson, 1982).

In order to provide the necessary structure, we have found it helpful to have the children rehearse their roles beforehand. For younger students, second and third graders, this entails providing them with the time to talk with one another in order to choose which characters are to be played by whom. They might also discuss what the essential dialogue might be, how the storyline is to unfold, and what it is they wish to get across to the audience. It might be beneficial to provide younger students with a list that outlines the main points of their rehearsal work. Such a list might include:

- What character are you playing?
- What are some important words to use?
- Do you have a beginning, middle, and an end?
- What is the main point of your role play?

Keeping them focused on some important elements while they rehearse should help them to stay on task and maximize the role play experience.

For older students, fourth grade and beyond, role play rehearsals can be structured by having students actually script their dialogue, either immediately prior to role playing or at some time after they have explored the how's and why's during the exploratory discussion session. The following is one scripted role play created by three fourth graders.

Sally:	Hey Samantha, I'm sorry I insulted you.
Samantha:	But why'd you insult me?
Sally:	I insulted you because Julie insulted me, so I insulted you to get my feelings out.
Samantha:	Let's go talk with Julie.
Sally:	Yeah.
Samantha:	Why did you insult Sally, Julie?
Julie:	Because I was angry. Hey, how about we take some time to be alone. That doesn't mean we can't be friends, it's just so we can cool down. So, what do you say?
Samantha:	O.K. I like it.
Sally:	O.K. I like it too.

In this scripted role play, the students are exploring one possibility as to the nature of arguments between friends. One friend has taken her aggression out on another friend due to misdirected anger. Though the story and the role play action are quite simple, these children have provided the audience with enough information for discussion and elaboration. Group discussion could revolve around how people come to know why they act as they do—"I insulted you to get my feelings out"—or how to resolve things when tempers get out of control—"how about we take some time to be alone … just so we can cool down." In addition, the group may wish to explore with more depth the reason behind Julie's initial anger toward Sally. Thus, by beginning with a script the children are allowed to present their ideas on relational problems clearly, with the focus being primarily on group discussion and understanding.

Because the children are just beginning to learn about the relationship tensions, it is particularly important during this first phase of role playing to focus discussions on the content of the enactments, and not the product. These scripted role plays, while not necessarily interesting from a dramatic perspective, offer a great opportunity to make connections between the student-created dialogues and the classroom discussions that took place when the students were first introduced to the tensions. In this sense, these role plays serve not so much as a means for students to inhabit a character for interpersonal discovery as they do to simply prepare them while they are learning the new language of the relationship tensions for more engaging work in the future.

This phase of role playing is also a good time for the teacher to begin to model for the students what sort of questions and analyses might be most beneficial. Role play discussions should be focused on the connection between the dialogue and the tension being portrayed. A teacher can help solidify understanding by asking the group questions such as:

- What did they do?
- What was the choice being portrayed?
- What would happen next?

And when the students have been introduced to the tensions more explicitly:

- How does this role play relate to the tension?
- Which character(s) was experiencing the tension? How?
- Were the characters experiencing the tension differently?
- Do you think the resolution would really work?

Questions such as these help to solidify the students' relational understanding by making clear connections between how they were defined during previous discussions and how they relate to their own representations. At the same time, the children will also broaden their comprehension of the tensions by witnessing the many different ways and the many different circumstances in which they can be portrayed.

Aside from making explicit connections to initial discussions, the teacher can also establish the atmosphere of the role play experience by providing guidelines for the audience to follow while discussing the action. van Ments, (1983) wrote of some techniques for debriefing after role playing that we have found very helpful:

- Address the players by their character names.
- Role players should try to respond as their character and not as themselves.
- Avoid remarks that speak to the quality of the performance.
- Emphasize the action that has occurred, and not alternative actions.
- Comments should be descriptive rather than evaluative.
- Role players should remain on the stage area.

Essentially, there are two aims behind these techniques. The first is to get the students used to seeing their classmates as others, as characters rather than themselves. This will help to establish the necessary distance between the students and their characters, which is essential in terms of them feeling safe enough to fully explore potentially sensitive issues. Thus, it is important for the audience to address their remarks to the character rather than the person. The second aim is to take the focus off the performance aspect of the role play and direct it towards the intent of the role play. Often it is the case when observing role plays that classmates desire to be entertained and their concentration towards the activity as a meaningful learning process is diminished (Stanford, 1974). As such, teachers should de-emphasize both the role players' need to entertain and the audience's expectation of entertainment. Both participation in and observation of the role play should be centered on the exploration of learning.

To summarize, the main points of this first phase of role playing revolve around:

- Building communication and dialogue skills.
- Building dialogue writing skill.
- Reducing performance anxiety.
- Strengthening relational understanding.
- Modeling audience expectations.
- Providing guidelines for student inquiry.

Development through these processes begins first by strengthening student abilities to create dialogue, then by alleviating the anxiety of performing in front of others, as well as making sure that the students have a clear understanding of how to enact and how to comment on their ideas. Once the children feel comfortable with their knowledge of how to present their thoughts, it might be time to move on to the next phase.

Phase 2: Role Playing–Imitative Range

Role Playing involves the existence of more individual variation. As Sternberg and Garcia pointed out, "Developmentally, when we learn a new role, we begin with role taking behavior. As we become more comfortable with the routines of the role, we move to role playing ..." (1989, p. 105). For example, a beginning teacher may be aware of the behaviors expected of her and will be a role taker, based on, say, how her mentor has performed these duties, and once comfortable with performing these tasks, she may become a role player as she begins to put more of her own way of doing things into these tasks. Another way to view role playing is its connection to the stage. It is like an actor who has permission to deviate from the script and rephrase dialogue into his or her own words while still being true to the original intention of the writer.

Sandberg's imitative range is much like role playing. It is "characterized by approval-seeking and somewhat superficial cooperation with the group ... (and individuals) may still have no real confidence or ability to effectively express the self" (1981, p. 37). A big difference from the stereotyping range, however, is that there is a greater intent of effort. Children may still be struggling, but it is because they are working towards finding their way in the role play process. As far as reflection is concerned, individuals in the imitative range generally offer either negative or positive responses and have difficulty elaborating on their experience.

We have found that after some time, typically after each tension has been role played once, students will lose interest in the role play if they continue to read from their scripts. Once they are familiar with the routine it is important to encourage more individual variation because too much structure will discourage learning (Johnson, 1982). Some of the ways that we have found to scaffold the children from reading from scripts to more fully inhabiting their characters is to have the students complete the presented story with their own narratives that describe in their own words the actions, thoughts, and feelings of the characters without necessarily providing them with dialogue. One such story, depicting the independence–dependence tension, was written by a fourth grader:

> Tim, John, and Sarah were best friends. They knew each other since kindergarten. Every Halloween they go trick-or-treating together. John doesn't really like going out because it's so cold. John got an invitation to a Halloween party from a person he plays soccer with. He told Tim and Sarah that he got an invitation to a party and he wasn't going to go trick-or-treating with them, even though he sort of wanted to go with his friends. Tim and Sarah got mad at him and said that they wouldn't speak to him again. John was sad and confused. John thought they were jealous and he ended up going to the Halloween party. The next day Tim and Sarah went to John and said sorry that they were being so rude to him and it was a bad thing to fight about it. So they were friends again.

In using this story, the role players have a recipe for feelings, attitudes, and the story line, but they don't have specific dialogue. When the students role play this scenario they have less structure and must decide how to portray each character's position as the action unfolds, relying on their own sense of the action.

Another scaffolding approach, which can be used in conjunction with the story writing or as a substitute, is to use worksheets that help focus the students on the pertinent aspects of the characters. One such worksheet is Table 4.1. It focused around a story about a student who refuses help from another student and was filled in by a fourth grader.

An advantage to using a worksheet like the aforementioned one is that unlike having the students write their own stories, the teacher can draw student attention to important elements that may have been absent from their stories. This worksheet was designed to get the children to focus on the motivations behind the actions by having the students supply a reason why a character feels a particular way. It is a way of broadening their perspectives, to get them to consider more heavily those elements that the teacher thinks are missing from the role plays or which the teacher feels are otherwise important. Based on observations of the role plays, the teacher may wish to tailor the worksheets in whichever way will best promote further learning.

Another such worksheet, Table 4.2, we've used, asks the students to explore both characters within the story.

For this worksheet, students have to consider two people's points of view, which helps to promote more complex considerations of the relationship situation. The specific aforementioned questions could be used for almost any story and tension, but teachers are encouraged to create their own questions according to classroom needs and interests. The idea here is to get the

TABLE 4.1
Role-Play Worksheet

Character's name:	Jim
How does he feel?	Jim feels jealous and dumb
Why does he feel that way?	He feels dumb because of how smart Fred is
How did he show his feelings?	By calling Fred a nitwit and hurting his feelings
What might have been a better way to express himself?	Jim could have said it in a nicer way and say, "No Thank you, I'd rather work alone."
What can he do now to change the situation?	He can say he is sorry and say I should have said something nicer.

TABLE 4.2

Role-Play Worksheet—Tensions

Sam and Jessica are friends. Sometimes Sam gets annoyed because Jessica tells him to do too many things that she likes to do. Sometimes Sam can't do them. Sam feels like he just can't tell Jessica that he sometimes feels she is annoying. Sam is not sure what to do.

Instrumentality–Affection

Goal: Balance the tension between liking someone because they do what you want and liking someone for who they are.

How does Jessica treat Sam?	How does Sam treat Jessica?
What are Jessica's feelings toward Sam?	What are Sam's feelings towards Jessica?
Why does Jessica feel–behave that way?	Why does Sam feel–behave that way?
What can she do to make it more balanced?	What can he do to make it more balanced?
Would you be her friend? Why or why not?	Would you be his friend? Why or why not?

students to realize that relationship problems are not always black and white, and that there may be no simple resolutions. It is important in this second phase of role playing that the students move away from creating nice, tidy representations that focus too heavily on unrealistic resolutions. One of the problems we have frequently encountered is a desire on the part of the students to make a speedy run through their role plays to get to "sorry, let's be friends again." Students need to be reminded during this second phase of role playing that resolutions are not always necessary. They should be working, instead, on exploring the antecedents and consequences of discord, while also developing novel ways to respond to, initiate, and talk about relationship issues.

Whereas role playing in the first phase (the scripting phase) centered around strengthening tension comprehension, setting expectations for the audience, introducing the students to portraying their thoughts dramatically, and allowing students to feel comfortable performing in front of others, this second role playing phase is concerned with getting the students to become more authentic in their actions, words, and sentiments and to become more immediately involved at the level of experiential feeling so that their portrayals become more like real life (Wright, 1984). Thus, having become adept at role taking through learning rudimentary role play skills and the essential ideas behind the relationship tensions, the students should now be ready to become role players, to respond, more or less, spontaneously in the moment. This means that the students are no longer required to portray a story line as much as they are to explore, in action, their own thoughts and perspectives through their alter egos, the characters.

Just as we've mentioned previously that the foundation of the RLC discussion process is centered upon the *why* question, which taps into inferential thinking and explanations for relational conflicts, the role playing in the second phase should concentrate on this as well. Only, rather than discussing ideas, the students are now called upon to present them dramatically. For example, in the previous worksheet example that dealt with the characters Jim and Fred, the explanation for the conflict was that Fred makes Jim feel jealous and dumb. A role play around this story could focus on how the children portray these states of mind in terms of the relationship. Thus, one of the aims of the players could be to show what a character looks like who is experiencing these feelings. How does he act? How does he react? Additionally, how does the role player feel having to portray a jealous character? How does the audience feel watching such a portrayal? The idea here is to have the students begin to experience, as characters, the very same explanations they themselves provided during discussion. Through inhabiting characters and their situations, the students (role players as well as audience) begin to make a more personal connection to the curriculum, thereby expanding their range of commitment and knowledge.

In order to accomplish this, new demands are put on the teacher in terms of facilitating the role plays. The teacher (and the students) must be willing to forego expectations that the role play being presented is a finished product (as it is in the first phase); it is, in fact, a work in progress. Rather than portraying a conflict and a resolution, it might be more beneficial to concentrate on the conflict and work towards the resolution as characters begin to understand each other's perspective through dialogue. Just as we hope that the students will notice as they progress through the curriculum that explanations for framing relational conflicts grow increasingly complex, as discussed in chapter 3, so do the possible ways in which these conflicts can or cannot be resolved. So the role plays in the second phase should concentrate on expanding student perception and portrayal of conflicts. It is a matter of providing another venue for which the students can make their implicit knowledge of their social world more explicit; therefore, heightening the level at which their knowledge can be analyzed, reconstructed, and/or affirmed by themselves and by the group.

The teacher, therefore, must take a more involved role in the action as a facilitator. At this point, after gleaning the collected interests, strengths, and difficulties of the group, the teacher will be in a position to notice when important issues arise during the role play. It is difficult to provide a prescribed mode of action in this area for two reasons. First, the specific agenda a teacher brings to the RLC will decide where he or she chooses to place the focus. Secondly, the way in which the students perceive and enact their relational understandings will be to a great degree determined by the nature of the children as a group. This means, in a sense, that as no two classrooms are alike, nor are the specific ways in which children react to one another in the classroom context alike. As well, the level of the students' understandings, their social and cognitive functioning, will be continually emerging.

Unlike the first phase of role playing, where the students have already scripted the action, this second role play phase is open to some new complications regarding the actual enactment. Some problems a teacher may encounter:

- A desire to entertain
- Rushing to a conclusion
- Repetition
- Poor performance
- De-roling

As mentioned earlier, the educational value of role playing can get lost if students are too concerned with entertaining their classmates. Though some students will undoubtedly create dialogues or write scripts in the first phase that are meant to get a laugh, the tendency to put on a comedic sketch in the second role play phase increases because the children are called on to be more spontaneous; as such, the students are exposed to feeling vulnerable or defensive.

Some children, feeling stuck, will fall back on silliness in order to make themselves more at ease. The problem when this arises is twofold. First, the student who is burlesquing is probably not getting much out of the experience. Second, the student who role plays for laughs is likely to disrupt both the intentions of the other players and the careful attention of the audience. We have found that a good way of handling these situations is to stop the role play and re-focus the student's efforts. If a student continues to have problems, the teacher may wish to have the student change roles with his or her partner, or to move on to the next role play. Making these determinations will depend largely on the teacher's knowledge of and rapport with the student in question. Questions a teacher may wish to consider are "Is it the circumstance of this particular role play that causes the student to act out?"; "Does the student tend to burlesque no matter the circumstances?"; "Is the student having a problem inhabiting a role because of social difficulties?" Based on the answers to these questions, the teacher can act according to his or her intuition on how to handle the problem. The important thing when interrupting a role play, moving on to another, or addressing a player out of character is to acknowledge the effort put forth by the students, thereby not diminishing the possibility for improvement.

Another problem students face when role playing is rushing to a conclusion. A possible reason for why students may do this relates to the same condition for the tendency to play for laughs. When students feel uncomfortable or stuck they sometimes just want to get it over with and leave the stage. A teacher may wish to have the players back up and focus on that aspect of the action that they have rushed through. If the students have rushed their role play because they simply were not prepared, the teacher might let it go. Again, it is up to the teacher to decide, based on his or her knowledge of individual students, how to react. We have found that often it is best to simply let the players end and begin the next role play. Students will have plenty of opportunities to develop their role play skills and their comfort levels; encouraging them to do something that they are not yet prepared may promote an effect quite opposite to the goal of the RLC—a disinterest in exploring the nature of social relationships.

General poor performance and repetition of dialogue could indicate many things. These problems, however, are typically quite different than the ones previously mentioned. We have found that when students are engaged in a lackluster role play or get stuck on dialogue, it is not that they are always unprepared or not ready for role play work, but that they may be uncertain as to their agenda. It could be an indication that the students are struggling with a complex issue. If this is the case, a teacher may wish to stop the role play and have a discussion with the players as to what it is they want to accomplish. Reconnecting them with the tension and the motivations of the characters might be a helpful way to get them back on track. The trick here for the teacher is being able to discern the amount of effort the students are bringing to their role plays. When students are making an earnest attempt to explore or portray an issue it is probably best to have them keep working at it even if they are struggling. The teacher needs to be tuned in to how the process is working for the students, rather than to how it looks as a performance. This can be, of course, difficult because the ability to intimate the experience of individual students takes time and evolves throughout the teacher–child and teacher–group relationship. Nonetheless, it has been our experience that teachers have the best vantage point from which to make such decisions.

De-roling is another factor that hampers the role play process. De-roling occurs when students get out of character and address the audience or the teacher as themselves. Typically, this happens when role players have made a mistake or have otherwise found themselves off-track. "Wait, let me start over," and "What I meant to do was ..." are common de-rolling occurrences. It also happens that students will de-role by addressing their partners, instructing them what to do, or pointing out errors. Unless a student persists in coming out of a role, there need not be any direction or intrusion necessary. We've often witnessed that role players will quickly recover from de-roling. They may simply ask to begin again or will catch themselves, continuing on as if they never left their role. If, however, a student displays a pattern of de-roling, the teacher must try to establish the reason for the role player's behavior. It might be that they are nervous, unprepared, or troubled by the complexity. As previously discussed, it is up to the teacher's discretion as to which actions to take.

Recapitulating, the main ideas behind this second role play phase concentrate upon:

- Utilizing worksheets
- Scaffolding spontaneity
- Focusing on the conflict rather than the resolution
- More teacher involvement in the action

Finally, a cautionary note:

> The (teacher) should always be aware of the temptation to 'play games' with the group and see 'what happens if ...'. It is vital to the success of the role play that it is taken seriously by the participants and that they regard the outcome as reasonable under the particular circumstances. If they do not then nothing will be learnt because they will regard the situation as an artificial one, completely controlled and manipulated by the (teacher) and therefore not a representation of reality. (Van Mentz, 1983, p. 109)

Though it may not always seem so through their performance, children typically bring a great amount of intrinsic motivation to role playing (Courtney, 1990). They may often become inhibited, but their desire to do well and present their unique perspectives in a role play scenario is usually quite strong. For this reason, it is important that the teacher find a balance between letting the students dictate how they are to make use of their role play time (through their abilities, knowledge, interests, and problems) and how much scaffolding and guidance is required for meaningful work.

Phase 3: Role Creating–Creative Range

Role Creating "permits the individual a high degree of freedom" (Moreno, 1953, p. 47). Continuing the teaching metaphor, it resembles the action of a teacher who, though having a well-formed plan of instruction, is able to respond to unexpected happenings, such as a poignant question posed by a student that leads the planned instruction in a different direction, or finding that the students are not receiving the lesson well, is able to redirect her teaching to meet student needs. Role creating on the stage might best be exemplified by the improvisational actor who brings a great deal of spontaneity and creativity to an ill-structured scene. Role creating is the ideal mode of action to be in because of its reliance on spontaneity and creativity, thus affording the greatest amount of reflection and learning.

Role creators might be thought of as working in Sandberg's (1981) creative and communicative range, which is marked in part by the ability of individuals to reflect and act in tandem. Students in this range are able to inhabit and portray a character while simultaneously reflecting on their own performance, thoughts, and feelings. Another way to look at it is to consider that students at this point are working at a higher level of meta-awareness.

At this level of action, role players are able to find new and creative ways of dealing with the world *in situ*. It is difficult to say whether or not students will actually be able to be role creators with any sort of consistency, since they are not being specifically trained for this purpose. However, in this third phase of role playing, we mean to steer the children in this direction. After the students, as a group, have shown proficiency with tension comprehension to the point that they have established a common language that they are continually re-working and have displayed adeptness at role playing, it may be time relinquish the structure that had been established in the second phase.

Now, after having utilized scripts, student-created narratives, and worksheets to help students frame their thoughts, the teacher may wish to do away with these and encourage the children to take a greater step towards improvising their role plays. Actually, it has been our experience that no matter how many different types of worksheets have been devised (in order to focus on different character aspects), the children will reach a point as a group where this external method for framing their perspectives ceases to be helpful.

As can be determined by the framework for the role play phases, one of the important processes is the gradual reduction of an external structure. The students, having now been exposed, and actively working with, the complexities of social relationships, should be ready to rely more strongly on their own intuitions and cognitive and emotional resources. Some prerequisites for this sort of work include being comfortable performing in front of others, being able to inhabit a character with little effort, and being able to draw on their knowledge of the relational tensions easily. It is up to the teacher's discretion on how to prompt the students for role play work in this third phase. A few techniques we have used include simply providing a tension, providing a time and a place, and leaving it entirely up to the students.

The advantage of letting the students decide for themselves or giving them vague conditions, is that the children now have less opportunity to censor their thoughts and feelings or have their actions imposed on them by the teacher (through the use of worksheets, etc.). They are forced, so to speak, into performing closer to their own personalities; and as such, it is hoped that their role plays become more truthful, more connected to the everyday experiences they have with their relationships.

The teacher's role as a facilitator during this phase is essentially the same as it is during the second role play phase, with the exception that, since there is now an increasing possibility that students will lose their way during performance, the teacher needs to be able know when to let the role play continue and when to interject. The difficulty in making these decisions lies in the fact that the teacher will not, because these role plays are not based on a common story, be privy to the students' conceptions and particular goals. Thus, just as the children will be elaborating their knowledge and skill throughout the curriculum, so must the teacher expand on his or her abilities to facilitate a more meaningful role play session.

Summary of the Developmental Phases

Table 4.3 outlines the general role play phases. Though these three types of roles and ranges can be to lesser or greater degrees present in an individual simultaneously during the same activity, they are considered to indicate the process by which one develops a repertoire of roles or abilities. First we learn the rudimentary, stereotypical aspects of a role (whether it be riding a bicycle, teaching a class, parenting a child, etc.). Once we are successful with these aspects we begin to deviate from the hard structure of the activity and insert our own individual touches. Finally, and hopefully, we become so competent in our understanding of the activity that we are able to transform it, creating a whole new way of thinking and behaving.

One can see how children may use any of these styles across any number of school activities. A role taker in math, for example, is one who given the directions on how to solve a division problem will do it just as instructed and rely on step-by-step examples. A role player in math might be who one who follows the directions but realizes that she can skip steps one and two because she can

TABLE 4.3
Role-Play Phases

Role play phase	Method	Focus	Goal
Phase I Role Taking	Dialogue rehearsal (younger students); scripted	Ideas & perspectives	Establish comfort; make links to tensions; model audience discussion
Phase II Role Playing	Worksheets, Student narratives	Role play action & conflict	Scaffold spontaneity & creativity
Phase III Role Creating	Improvising	Role play action, conflict & resolution	Encourage more truthful, personal enactments

do them in her head. A role creator in math might be one who, fully cognizant of how the steps to a division problem operate, finds a new way to solve the problem altogether. We can notice, too, that the particular assumptions a child brings to these tasks about his or her own efficacy may have a strong effect on how comfortable he or she is to be spontaneous and creative. One who feels that she or he is poor in math may strive to "do it by the book." One who feels her or his math skills are good may be able to push herself or himself to a new level of comfort and take some risks. The student who feels quite proficient may risk even more. It works no differently when it comes to the RLC role play; there needs to be a combination of knowledge gained through learning about relationships and a strong, developing efficacy about presenting and examining this knowledge in a novel way.

Different children bring different experiences and comfort levels to the act of performing in front of others, especially when the performance can, at times, seem to be quite personal and revealing. For this reason, when we talk about students being role takers, role players, or role creators, we mean not only to point to an individual's state of readiness or spontaneity in the traditional sense of Moreno (1953), but also to other traits such as abilities for verbalizing, writing, working together, problem-solving skills, and general understanding of the material that has been discussed in other parts of the RLC. All of these things can impact on how well (in terms of performance and learning) a student is able to role play.

It is probably best when introducing the children to role playing to assume that all students, regardless of grade level, will be in the role-taking stage. Though some students might bring unique experiences with them that show a strong penchant for spontaneity, and acting or interpersonal awareness, unfamiliarity with the goals of the curriculum and teacher expectations will make it difficult for students to gain from the role play experience. As well, even though some students might feel comfortable role playing, it is important to remember that the learning experience comes primarily not from the product or performance, as it does from the process—the ability of the student to be able to inhabit and portray a role while also being able to reflect on it. The idea is not to be acting in the theater sense of the term, but to be immediately involved in the action to the degree that new understandings can arise. Given this, a good amount of structure is necessary when introducing the role plays into the curriculum.

Other Considerations

In order to assure the quality of the role play process, the teacher must be aware of some further elements that may be problematic or helpful:

- Warming up the group
- Providing closure
- Choosing partners
- Journaling

One of the most discussed aspects of successful role playing centers on warming-up the group prior to the enactment (Blatner, 1988; Courtney, 1990; Moreno, 1953). The purpose of warming up for role plays is really no different than any other sort of preparation one undertakes before beginning a complex activity; and individuals may vary on what constitutes a warming-up process for them. In the RLC, we have found that the most important aspect is simply allowing the children time to prepare. This means that they should be allowed to rehearse (in the first phase) and discuss their aims with one another (in the second and third phases). In order to provide support and direction, the teacher may wish to check in with the students during their warming-up to answer questions, clear up misunderstandings regarding the task, and perhaps offer suggestions to those who are having difficulty formulating their ideas. As well, we have found that many children need encouragement, affirmation, and praise while they are preparing so as to minimize anxiety and uncertainty. The main point is to assure that the students are ready to portray their characterizations. If they are unprepared it is unlikely that the role playing will be successful.

Providing closure is also very important. Closure doesn't mean that a solution has been found or a conflict has been resolved, rather it points to making enough time for the role players to have finished their work and for the audience to have engaged in a discussion of the enactment. For the teacher, it means summarizing the experience for the class and pointing out those elements or themes that he or she will want to focus on in the future. It is important for the teacher to leave enough time for group reflection, since discussions centered around the role plays are just as valuable as the role plays themselves. Some things to watch for are making sure that the role players have had the opportunity to answer questions from the audience, to clarify their intent during discussion, or both. It is one thing for students to have opposing opinions on how something should or should not have happened during a role play (or the ideas behind it), but if the players are refrained from responding then a teacher risks diminishing student motivation for exposing themselves and their perspectives in the future. It may be helpful to keep in mind that though the children are portraying characters, it is often the case that they are putting a great deal of themselves (consciously or unconsciously) into their role plays. Thus, it is not a good idea for the teacher to leave the impression that a role play was unimpressive or otherwise unworthy of comment.

Another element of the RLC that can only be determined by the individual teacher, is that of choosing role play partners. During the first and second phases of the role play, students probably need to know ahead of time who they are working with so they can construct their dialogues, create narratives, and complete worksheets. In the beginning a teacher may wish to allow the students to pick their own partners, thereby increasing the chance that they will feel comfortable in their work. Throughout the curriculum, as the teacher begins to see the various strengths and weaknesses in role playing, it might be a good idea to assign partners according to ability. We have often found that pairing children who are of similar proficiency makes for the best learning experience. It may also be the case that stronger role players can raise the performance of less motivated students when they work together, as long as there isn't too much of a gap between ability levels. Thus, students who are in the role-taking stage may work successfully with those in the role playing stage, but probably not as well with those children who are in the role creating range. Another aspect for teachers to consider is to make use of emerging or perpetual conflicts that exist in the classroom. Based on a teacher' s insight into the social world of the students, role players might be assigned for the purpose of working out real-life problems. This can be potentially hazardous, but teachers who have good instincts about the maturity level of the students should take advantage of the role play process as an opportunity to create real change in the classroom community. Finally, though it is difficult to recommend a prescription for how many students should be involved in a role play, we have found that it should not be more than two or three. Even when a teacher uses a story with more characters, it might be helpful to scale them down. If students have superfluous roles they probably will not gain much from the experience, and it has often been the case that when too many people are involved the performance tends to get chaotic.

One last consideration to make is that of encouraging students to keep a role-play journal. Such a journal should be concerned with a student's private reflections. Though all students should have the opportunity to share their views during discussion, there may still be much that a child would not share, and maybe should not share, with the group. Journals might focus on personal reflections and discoveries of how it feels to role play in a specific situation or relational context. As well, it might include a progress report of sorts, allowing for students to reflect on the more technical aspects of the role play such as how it could have been improved and what seemed to really work.

CONCLUSIONS

This chapter elucidated the basic process for role playing within the curriculum, which we feel should be a good starting point for teachers when first attempting to implement dramatic activities. We began with a discussion of Moreno's (1953) theory of how individuals take on and develop their role repertoire and how his techniques and those of educational dramatists can be integrated into the RLC in a manner that supports the objectives of this curriculum. Furthermore, we have touched upon incidents that may arise during role play sessions. These serve as just a few of the many spontaneous developments that may occur, and for which teachers should be prepared.

Teachers should feel free to consult the worksheets in the appendix to further help guide them through the role playing process, and to adapt them to their own needs and interests. Facilitating role plays can be difficult and overwhelming at times, but it is well worth the effort. Many children bring a great amount of excitation and motivation to these activities, and the work that the children do with the stories and in discussion can be supported and enhanced through role playing. It is an opportunity for students to explore, share, and display their knowledge in a novel, fun way.

5

Shifting Responsibility Within the Relational Literacy Curriculum: Making Conceptual Connections

"The rubberband is kind of like ... every time you do something fun with your friend, that strengthens the rubberband and makes it harder for it to snap."

INTRODUCTION

Prior to the final two sessions of the basic cycle of the curriculum, the children have participated in four problem-solving discussions and role plays, each highlighting a different relational tension. At this point, the group should have a good feel for the process and can begin to take more ownership of it. Teachers should also feel more automatic with their prompts and where they want to direct the children's thinking through the discussions and role plays. Consequently, teachers can begin to shift more responsibility to their students for directing the course of the curriculum. This is an important step and one that is neces-

83

sary to take if the RLC is to be truly effective. As children take greater ownership of what is discussed and how the discussions take place, they come to see the process as something they can own and use.

To take more responsibility in the RLC, children need a conceptual framework from which to organize their experience and better anticipate events. A conceptual framework allows children to more effectively make decisions about what is important and how to respond; to remember and learn from their experience and their reflections on experience; and to critique their own thinking and action. A conceptual framework provides a vantage point from which to examine and question taken-for-granted ways of relating. As children internalize a conceptual framework for aiding their understanding of relationships, they can take greater responsibility in directing their own learning.

In this chapter, we outline three ways to help children construct a conceptual framework within the RLC. Indeed, there may be many more and teachers may well improvise. The three ways we suggest all focus on making the dialectical tensions explicit and connecting the children's own linguistic concepts with these new concepts.

The general model for the exercises we introduce in this chapter is represented in Fig. 5.1. The essential idea is to help children build a conceptual framework by making links between the stories they discuss and experience, their own language for these stories, and the language–concepts of the four tensions. In making these links, they are forging new concepts and organizing them in ways to better interpret the dynamics of relationships. The really novel dimension within this model is that of the dialectic tensions. By introducing these and incorporating them into the child's way of conceptualizing interpersonal events, they have a new way of framing them, and a way that is explicit to them. This is the goal of the activities we introduce in this chapter.

BUILDING A CONCEPTUAL FRAMEWORK

In this chapter, we outline three distinct ways of supporting the children's development of a conceptual framework. These activities essentially forge mental links between the children's own

Child Language   Tensions

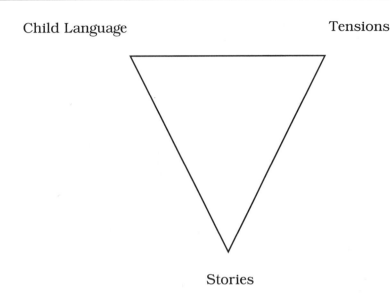

Stories

FIG. 5.1.   Conceptual connections framework.

language for relating, the stories, and the dialectic tensions. We introduce them in the order in which they are most useful to introduce to the children.

Defining the Four Tensions With the Children

We offer two activities aimed at helping the children become aware of the relational tensions that can underlie the peer conflicts they encounter. Defining the tensions is critical for the students to develop their framework. Up to this point in the curriculum process, the tensions have been something only the teacher has used in constructing or choosing the stories. There has been no emphasis on defining them or pointing them out to the children. Following the basic cycle of the four stories, the teacher can introduce the four tensions and begin to explicitly use them as a way to guide the children's reflections.

Writing Their Own Stories

Once the four tensions have been defined and discussed through one of the activities, we suggest that the children write stories of their own that illustrate the four tensions. This can serve as a check of their understanding of the tensions as well as a source of further material for the discussion–role play process.

Concept Mapping of Key Terms

The children introduce their own language that powerfully reflects their experience in relationships. It is important to listen for these terms and pull them out for all students to appreciate. In this way, the group begins to construct a shared language for feelings and events that can be challenging to put into words. We share one example of a powerful term that children used for relational conflicts and illustrate it through a concept mapping technique that can also be used with children to clarify their thinking around complex ideas.

EXPLORING THE DIALECTIC TENSIONS

Why Make the Tensions Explicit?

As we previously noted and in earlier chapters, the tensions can serve as the basis for a conceptual framework that will help children focus on interactions in relationships. They help us to see the dynamics of communication rather than only noting the personality characteristics of a single individual. The tensions framework provides a way for the children to elaborate and refine their understanding of friendships and other relationships, the first goal of the RLC.

Aren't the Tensions Too Difficult for Children to Comprehend?

Although the concepts are challenging and abstract, we have been successful in helping children to understand them by forming connections between the tensions and their own terms and concepts for relating. We recommend two activities that we have used to introduce the tension concepts to the students; a story-sorting task and a vocabulary-story matching activity. Through activities such as these, the children connect the familiar with the novel to expand their understanding. They also achieve the second goal of the curriculum by developing a common language with which to share and clarify their social experiences.

How Can the Children Really Use These Concepts to Think About Their Interactions?

In applying the tensions, the notion of balance becomes important. Why is it important to have both judgment and acceptance or independence and interdependence in friendship? The children can understand how relating involves both poles of a tension when they use the notion of balance. This typically becomes the focus of discussion once the individual terms have been explored. Pushing the discussion beyond simple sharing and definitions of terms is important in accomplishing the third goal of the curriculum, to articulate, explore, and critique group norms.

STORY-SORTING TASK

The story-sorting exercise occurs after the four hypothetical stories representing each of the tensions have been discussed and role played. In this activity, the children work in small groups to match two sets of stories. One set includes the four stories that they have already been discussed and role played. The other set includes four novel stories that parallel the familiar stories in terms of the problem or tension in the story. The children are to pair the stories in terms of problem similarity and to record their reasons as to why they are similar on index cards provided to them. In this way, they come up with their own terms for the nature of the problem in the stories. Appendix B contains example parallel stories used in the sorting task written by tension. Table 5.1 contains a summary of materials and a set of directions for the small group activity.

Once the small groups have completed the story-matching task and recorded their own reasons for each pair, a large group-sharing discussion occurs. Through this discussion the children's story pairs along with their reasons are elicited and recorded on the board. In this way, the collective ideas of the entire class are organized in one list. Table 5.2 contains an example chart that was completed through this discussion. We recommend filling in

TABLE 5.1
Small Group Story-Matching Task

Materials: Four stories discussed in class

Four new but parallel stories

Four index cards

Directions to the small groups:

Each group has two sets of stories and four index cards. One set of stories includes the four stories we discussed this year. The other set includes four new stories. Work in your group to match the stories. Put each of the old stories with one of the new stories. Match it to the one that is most similar to it in terms of the problem in the story. You should end up with four pairs of stories. You have four index cards. Put each pair under an index card and write down an explanation of the similarity or a name for each of your pairs.

the story sort chart categories as the discussion occurs. The stories could either be represented by actually putting a large print version of the story on the board or some short hand for a particular story such as the characters' names. Recording the children's own terms in the key words section is a critical step as this will provide the linking of ideas to the tension terms.

The challenge in this discussion is to link the children's own phrases and labels for the categories to the dialectic tensions that we wish them to learn. This requires careful listening, quick thinking, and improvisation on the teacher's part. The children's own language typically contains aspects of the tensions and it's useful to help the children make these connections between what is familiar to them and the new ideas. Once the children's pairs and terms are up on the board, the teacher draws the group's attention to the tension term and elicits their ideas about what each term means. The children usually have some ideas. After definitions for each term are formed, we ask them to think about each term in relation to the two stories. How do they fit? It is in this process that the group typically works from their own terms to the new terms we have defined together.

TABLE 5.2
Story-Sort Chart

Old Story	New Story Match	Key Words	Tension Labels
		"Children's Language"	
Judgment–Acceptance Story	Novel J–A Story	"alone" "needs a friend"	Judgment–Acceptance
Expressive–Protective Story	Novel E–P Story	"have argument" "say no"	Expressive–Protective
Independent–Dependent Story	Novel I–D Story	"first they were friends but not now" "break up"	Independence–Dependence
Instrumentality–Affection Story	Novel I–A Story	"confused about the friendship" "turned his back on friend"	Instrumentality–Affection

In the following sets of excerpts, we show examples of the ways teachers can summarize children's ideas, questions, and help them connect their ideas to the dialectic tensions. The first example focuses on the judgment–acceptance tension.

Teacher: How is the acceptance–judgment theme part of those two stories? If judgment involves judging, evaluating people, holding your friend up to some standard, then acceptance is letting go of those standards, not paying attention to them, and just liking them and not judging them.

Teacher: Remember the things we said as a group, they both were being left out. They're both alone. They don't have friends.

Child: I know one for Elly, like Elly's being judged the way she is by the other group and they don't want her. They're judging the way she is and not accepting her.

Teacher: Okay, they're judging her and not accepting her. They say no to her and they didn't want her to play. So the judgment–acceptance tension was out of balance here.

Here we see a brief exchange that followed the discussion of the children's story pairs and definition of the terms judgment and acceptance. The teacher first directs the children to apply the terms to the two stories they paired while reminding them of the definitions. She then reiterates their terms for the similarity in the stories. This seemed to help one child make the connection that the girl who is alone and without friends is perhaps being judged by the others rather than accepted. The teacher further points out that the tension of judgment–acceptance is out of balance, meaning that there is too much judgment and not enough acceptance here. We return to the issue of balance in the following tension.

Teacher: So how do you think independence and dependence fit with our stories?

Teacher: Look at the things on the board and what we
           said about them. Somebody in each story
           makes a new friend. So then they have less time
           to spend with their old friend and they spend
           more time with a different person. And then the
           old friend is feeling left out and the friendship is
           falling apart. How do these ideas relate to the
           independence and dependence terms?

Child: Um … what was her name … the one where you
           really don't want to like go away from them, you
           just want to go away from them for a short pe-
           riod of time, because you've been together for a
           while.

Teacher: Which story did you see that one in?

Child: Um … Jack, Max, and …

Teacher: Elliot. Yes, they have been friends for years and
           this year Elliot started to draw away from them
           and go with other people. So you think he's
           kind of feeling that way? He's been friends with
           them for so long and now he's kind of pulling
           away from those guys to go be friends with
           some other people. Yes, that's an example of the
           independence–dependence dilemma.

Teacher: Do you guys think that it's good to have one or
           the other or to have both independence and de-
           pendence in a friendship? What do you think?

This excerpt within the independence–dependence discussion follows a similar pattern to our first example. The teacher
directs the children to link their terms to the new terms to the dilemmas in the stories. She ends with a thought provoking question about the issue of balance with the independence–dependence tension. The children go on to offer their opinions on this.

Child: Um, well kind of both, because sometimes I
           want to play with them and sometimes I like to
           play with somebody new.

Teacher: Okay, and how do you feel?

Child: I feel like I just need both of them.

Teacher: Kind of need both of them, how come?

Child: Because somehow I just don't want to play and then other times I feel like I want to play with others.

Teacher: So you kind of feel like you need a balance.

We can see in this brief exchange, the children begin to explore the notion of balance with the tension concept. They can see that an overabundance of one or the other pole can lead to problems. This is essentially the way we want them to begin to think about conflict. If they can begin to identify the tensions involved in a particular interpersonal conflict and the nature of the imbalance, they can then begin to better imagine the type of interpersonal negotiation that may be important to resolving the situation. It is this set of discussions that lays the framework for children and the beginnings of their understandings about the dialectic tensions. A teacher must remember that this is only a beginning of discussion about the tensions.

Through the small group story-matching task, the students have an opportunity to begin to define the tensions using their own experiences and student language. It is important to key into the student's own language and to also realize that the teacher plays a critical role in scaffolding this experience. Just as in the discussion process, the prompts and clarifications the teacher provides are critical to the success of this task. A teacher must be a good listener and tune into students' comments and the ensuing discussion.

VOCABULARY-STORY MATCHING ACTIVITY

An alternative to the story-matching task is a vocabulary-story matching activity. This exercise works in a very similar way, but without the introduction of novel stories. Following the completion of the four stories involving each of the four tensions, the teacher reflects over the scripts generated by the children. Recall that the scripts are the notes recorded as the group answered the three basic problem-solving questions for a story. The goal of this teacher reflection is to pull out language the children used to capture the tension or the interpersonal dilemma in the story. Similar to the story-sorting discussion previously described, the children's own terminology and concepts are the starting point in defining the tensions.

Once key terms have been identified, the teacher creates a reflection sheet. The purpose of this sheet is to provide structure for the children to reflect upon and respond to the meaning of the terms. At times, the terms children generate can be quite powerful metaphors for relationships and relational challenges. For example, as one group of children discussed a story involving the independence–dependence tension, they came up with the notion that friendship can be described as a rubberband. It ought to be flexible and expandable to accommodate change, but sometimes it can be stretched too far and it can break. The power of this metaphor for the children was clear in the number of times they referenced it through out the school year as they discussed different situations (Salmon & Freedman, 1999). We discuss the significance of children's metaphor more in the final section of this chapter. Most of the time, however, the terms children use to describe the conflicts in the stories are less poetic but no less important in making the connection to the dialectic tensions. Common language describing friendship challenges include some of the following terms:

Fake friendship

Being used

Breaking up

Wearing out

Growing apart

Being left out

Exploding

Telling a white lie

Trust

Jealousy

The important point here is to identify language that the children use, language that is meaningful to them, and language that captures the essential dilemma in a conflict. These terms are then used to create a think sheet to begin a discussion of the four dialectic tensions. Table 5.3 contains an example think sheet.

Each phrase on this think sheet can be associated with one of the four tensions. "Friendship is like a rubberband" relates to the independence–dependence tension. "Friendship is really just about the game" relates to the instrumentality–affection tension. "Someone feeling excluded" relates to the judgment–acceptance tension. "Someone telling a white lie" relates to the expressive–protective tension. Each indicated a way of describing conflict, and can be linked to an imbalance in one of the four

TABLE 5.3
Children's Relationship Terms Think Sheet

What do these sentences mean to you?

Which stories that we discussed do they make you think about? Why?

Friendship is like a rubberband.

Friendship is just really about the game.

Someone feels excluded.

Someone told a white lie to a friend.

tensions. For example, "feeling excluded" might reference a situation where someone feels overly judged or unfairly judged. Similarly, friends "growing apart" may signal an overly independent way of relating that may eventually erode the relationship altogether. Telling a "white lie" differs slightly from the others in that it refers to a strategy to maintain balance in the expressive–protective tension. When issues are minor, rather than express the truth, friends may choose to protect the other's feelings rather than being direct.

Once the children have completed their written vocabulary reflections, the teacher asks the group to share their thinking. Through this discussion, shared definitions of these concepts are created as well as shared associations to the stories. These can be displayed on a chart or thinking map showing the children's vocabulary and the associated story. Such visual displays help children organize and make explicit their problem definitions. A circle–square map, such as the example in Fig. 5.2, might be helpful in this regard (Hyerle, 1996).

At this point, the tension terms are introduced and added to the chart. Similar to the story-sorting task, the group first defines each term separately and then considers them together in terms of maintaining a balance in a friendship. It is important to help the children think about both elements within a tension and the importance of each in maintaining healthy communication in relationships. Some thought-provoking conceptual prompts that can help the children consider the complexity include the following:

- Is there ever a time to judge your friends? What would that be like?

- Is it ever possible to show too much affection? What would that be like?

- Is there ever a time for a friendship to just to be about the game or the activity your involved in together? What would that be like?

- Can friendships be limited to one kind of activity (e.g., football friends) or place (e.g., camp friends)?

Jill, Molly, and Ellen's Story

- Friendship is like a rubberband
- Expecting someone to be there
- Counting on a friend
- Needing your friend
- Free to decide about friendships

Independence–Dependence Tension

FIG. 5.2.   Circle/Square map.

- Is there a time to be independent in a friendship? What would that be like?

- Is it possible to point out something negative about a friend in a nice way?

Questions like these help children to consider how to balance the tensions in their communications with friends, and also to consider the side of the tension that sometimes isn't honored as explicitly. A word of caution is important here, however. Patterns in regard to relating are influenced by social, cultural, and developmental factors. Patterns of behavior that are most acceptable in friendships will vary from classroom community to classroom community. They could also vary between the teacher and the student, or between different groups of students within the same classroom. Indeed, cultural variation in acceptable patterns can be the source of conflict between students. Clearly the cultural backgrounds of the students as well as gender and developmental level make a difference in the patterns that are most prevalent and most accepted in their friendships.

It would be important for teachers to pay attention to the variations within the classroom in regard to the acceptable patterns. How directly do the children communicate in their peer relationships? What is acceptable within this community? How interdependent are they in relating? How independent? How directly do they show affection? What are their goals in relating to one another? How do they indicate their limits or boundaries with one another? A teacher's sensitivity to these patterns is important in planning conceptual prompts that might expand the children's awareness and thinking, and at the same time, honor important cultural values. Recall that one of the goals of the RLC is to articulate, explore, and critique group norms. Through RLC discussions, teachers gain access to the children's point of view. A careful examination of the values the children espouse, how these relate to their interactions with one another, and the teacher's own values and assumption are important to attend to in the process. As with all curricula, the teacher must make decisions about how to balance her values and those of her students.

ENGAGING CHILDREN IN WRITING THEIR OWN RLC STORIES

Once the tension concepts and terms have been introduced and connected to the stories that have been discussed, we engage the children in writing their own stories. Writing provides another vehicle to connect the meaning of the tensions to experience. Children generate their own relationship stories–dilemmas in the writing process, and either before or after writing, relate them to the tension concepts. In this way, the children further elaborate their conceptual framework.

The writing can be introduced in different ways. A teacher may simply brainstorm friendship issues or themes with the students eliciting ideas they could write about. In our own brainstorming, we found that children identify very important issues. Some examples we have encountered include the following:

- Getting along in a group.
- When friends change and grow apart.
- When a friend's reaction to us is hurtful.
- When classroom compositions change at the start of a new year.
- When a group of friends splits off into smaller groups, creating clicks of friends.
- When someone takes your best friend away.
- When friends are mean and grouchy.
- When friends brag a lot.

As the children generate topics, the teacher records them on the board or large chart paper. Following the brainstorming, we ask the children to choose the topic they wish to write a story about. The children can write individually or in a collaborative writing group. We have found the group writing to be particularly fruitful as the stories tend to more elaborate or complex. We then collect the children's stories and use them for the discussion and role plays in the second half of the school year. The following are examples of stories organized by tension that our students wrote in collaborative groups.

Judgment–Acceptance

At recess Pat is sitting by herself. Pat wants someone to play with. All the other kids are busy playing sports. She feels excluded. Pat doesn't know what to do. Pat feels lonely.

Mike and Ben hated each other, but their mothers were friends. So one day the moms went out and left them at home. And if they got along, both of them would get to go to Dairy Queen.

Independence–Dependence

One day four friends were playing soccer. Caitlyn said, "Jenny let's do some art inside." "No let's play barbies," whined Kelly.

"Barbies," screamed Jenny. "Caitlyn and Helen you like barbies!" "You're a baby." "Ah shut up," answered Kelly with dignity. And with that they all split up. But at that moment, Helen was wondering how to keep this friendship going.

Clinton and Bob were good friends. They knew each other since kindergarten. In first grade, Roosevelt came and took Bob away from Clinton, and Clinton couldn't play with Bob. Through second and third grade, Roosevelt took over Bob. Clinton got very frustrated.

Once there were two kids named D.J. and Taylor. The two kids are friends and they have frequent fights. One day D.J. wanted to play T-ball but Taylor wanted to play soccer. So they got into a fight. They both were wondering why they were getting in another fight. Then they realized that their friendship was suffering due to the many fights they were having.

Expressive–Protective

One day Pat and Jamie were talking. Then Pat said, "I just got Nintendo 64." "That's nothing compared to what I have," Jamie bragged back. Pat said, "Well, what do you have?" Jamie said, "I'm not telling—come over this weekend." Jamie got 64, Sega, and Nintendo. On Saturday, Pat came over, and said, "Where is the thing that is better than my Nintendo 64?" Jamie said, "In my room." Then Pat goes to Jamie's room and looks around and sees a 64, Sega, and Nintendo. "Oh no," Pat thought, "this has to stop, but what should I do?"

One day a few people were playing in the field. Then Brad comes along and says, "Let's play football." Chance, Jesse, and Jerry wanted to play in the field. Brad said, "Well I do, so come on!" They said, "No, we want to play in the field." Brad said, "If you don't play football, I'm not gonna play with you."

After my friend Ben came over I sort of regretted it. First he took the truck that I had lost (for days) and started playing with it. And when my mom offered us cookies he ate the whole thing. He didn't even give me a crumb. And when he went home he said: "See you Alex. I had fun. I loved the cookies. Did you like them too Alex?" He acted like he let me eat some. What a blow out!

Instrumentality–Affection

One day Sam, Jack, and Matilda were playing baseball in Jack's yard when, all of a sudden, Jack broke the window. "Uh oh," said Sam. Then Jack's mom came out the door and said, "Who in the world did this?" "Matilda," said Jack simply. "Well Matilda Birdman, go back to your house and tell your parents what you did!" "I DID NOT DO IT," said Matilda, "JACK DID!" "Yeah right," said Jack's mom. "Ha, ha, I fooled my mom. Now you get all the blame," and with that he walked in to his house to have his supper. "I HATE YOU," yelled Matilda. "A LOT!" she added. "I don't blame you," said Sam. "He gave you a bad reaction." "You can say that again," said Matilda. And they walked home to have their supper.

In discussing the child stories, we followed the same process described in chapter 3 with one exception. As the problem was defined, we asked the children about the tensions in the story. In each of the example aforementioned topics, one can imagine the influence of one or more of the four tensions. Typically, in the real situations that the children generate, more than one tension is relevant, however. Hence, we also encourage the children to begin to think about how the tensions relate. In this way, the children have more opportunities to make connections between the tension concepts and their own experience.

An alternative to brainstorming topics is simply to ask the children to generate stories that illustrate each of the four tensions. This exercise can also serve as an assessment of their understanding. How well do they understand and apply the tension to their own experience? Which tensions do they have more difficulty with? Where do more of their relational challenges lie? The stories generated here can be used for the discussion role play process in the second half of the year.

CONNECTION MAKING AND CONCEPT MAPPING

In paying close attention to the children's language and capturing terms that work for them, powerful connections can occur. To close this chapter, we share the connections that children made through the repeated use of a metaphor throughout one academic year of RLC discussions.

Friendship Is Like a Rubberband

The boys introduced "rubberband" as a metaphor for friendship in the first independence–dependence story we discussed in the fall of one year. They repeated the rubberband metaphor during our discussion of the next story, an instrumentality–affection theme. After explicitly linking the meaning of this metaphor to the independence–dependence tension through the vocabulary matching activity in early December, the class went on to use this metaphor in all subsequent independence–dependence stories occurring during the remainder of the year. In addition, they referred to the rubberband metaphor in a discussion of an actual conflict occurring among friends in the classroom that involved the independence–dependence tension (Salmon & Freedman, 1999). Table 5.4 contains a summary of the RLC discussion history in which the rubberband metaphor arose. (During this particular academic year, we had the boys and girls meeting separately in the fall as they learned the process in order to allow for smaller groups. We separated by gender as this was the nature of the classroom friendships. In the second half of the year, we met as a whole class.)

The children used the rubberband metaphor to provide a relational explanation for the conflict in a story as opposed to an explanation based upon either of the characters in the story, their circumstances, their differences, or concrete interactions

TABLE 5.4
Sequence of Discussions in Which Rubberband Metaphor Occurred

1. Boys discussion of independence–dependence story (10/17/96)
2. Boys discussion of instrumentality–affection story (11/12/96)
3. Whole class reflection session on tensions and child terms (12/3/96)
4. Child-authored independence–dependence story (2/18/97)
5. Discussion of real conflict among a group of boys (2/25/97)
6. Child-authored independence–dependence story (3/5/97)

(recall our categories of explanation introduced in chapter 3). We have found that metaphors are often used to provide relational explanations of conflict. Figure 5.3 contains a concept map essentially summarizing five fairly distinct relational ideas the children drew out of this metaphor and discussed in order to help them explore and explain the conflicts in the stories we discussed.

The boys introduced the metaphor emphasizing the notion of "two people pulling on the rubberband" (strand number 1). In this discussion, they highlighted the tension between two people in a relationship as one or both pulled in different directions. They noted that the relationship could "snap," if you pull too hard. The children went on to talk about a need to "let go" of the rubberband "slowly." "Letting go" of a rubberband referred to letting go of the friendship. When questioned further about why friendship could be thought of as a rubberband, the notion of "stretching" seemed key.

The children elaborated the significance of stretching in friendship in further discussion. This notion defined their second major line of thinking depicted in the map. They used the stretch in rubberbands to talk about both their community of friends and their relationship with a single individual being able to stretch and grow. A stretchable community was one in which more and "more friends" could be added. This could be "more fun," but also "hard to keep to yourself." Similarly, they talked about a small rubberband growing larger as one's friendship became stronger. In one exchange, the children talked almost simultaneously about a single friendship and a community of friends. With this dual focus they seemed to implicitly acknowledge the tensions between their dyadic friendships and their membership in the larger classroom community of friends. This is an issue they return to and more explicitly explore in a later discussion. The children also suggested that stretch within friendship allowed for "fighting and making up" and also allowed the relationship to grow and change. In particular, "playing together strengthens the rubberband." They referred to the thickness of the rubber band to represent the strength of the relationship.

The third and fourth strand in the rubber band map represent fairly closely related lines of thinking. The children offered

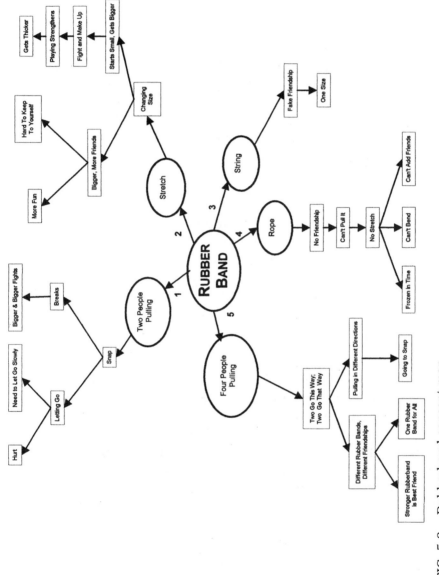

FIG. 5.3.   Rubberband concept map.

103

contrasting metaphors to the rubber band. The "string" signaled a "fake friendship" existing in only one size or overly based on instrumentality and lacking in affection. Changing its shape and size without fundamentally destroying it was central to what seemed important to the children about friendship. Similarly, the rope came to signal "no friendship" at all. The children explicitly recognized the need for flexibility and change in relationships, but at the same time, they saw the significance of connection. This seemed to be what made the rubberband metaphor so meaningful to them.

In the final line of discussion related to the rubberband metaphor, the children further developed the dynamics of a community of friends. Here the children recognized what can happen when more than two people are involved. There can be more than one rubberband and it can be pulled in many directions. The children began to use the rubberband image to help them think about relationships within groups. The reference to pulling in different directions captured some of the complexity of their experience.

This example provides an illustration of the potentialities when teachers pay attention to and encourage children's creative use of language. One generative metaphor helped make many important connections explicit and concrete. Indeed, the children found the metaphor so compelling, they returned to it throughout the year to help them articulate and describe qualities of relationships. We observed that in using this tool, the children constructed new ways of envisioning friendship problems. Educational researchers have recognized metaphor as an important cognitive tool for learners to facilitate their understanding as they construct a conceptual framework in a new domain (Ortony, 1993; Schon, 1993). By drawing on and applying a more familiar knowledge base, learners can gain insights into novel concepts. In this example, the image of a rubberband gave the students a familiar and useful tool for talking about and interpreting friendship dilemmas.

It is also important to note that the children's own language in this example moved them outside of the specifics of one story to think more abstractly about the challenges of friendship. As they used the notion of a rubberband they moved from a concrete focus on specific characters and their actions to a focus that emphasized more general principles of relating. They made their own assumptions explicit and understandable to each other. Taking a concept map such as the one we constructed here back to the children to review would be extremely helpful in this process. In this way, the children would have a visual organizing tool to help them remember the abstract connections they made. Linking the tension concepts and discussing how their concrete images of stretching and pulling relate to the independence–dependence notion would be most helpful as children build a conceptual framework for relationships.

In linking the children's language, the four tensions, and stories or experiences of conflict, the children can gradually construct a conceptual framework or mental map for relationships. Such a cognitive tool provides a platform for thinking inside and outside of specific instances of relating. With different conceptual vantage points from which to view conflict, children may begin to see that they have choices and make better decisions regarding their actions in future conflict situations.

6

Working With Children's Real Conflicts

"Every year our friendship changes ..."

INTRODUCTION

Our interpersonal relationships are inherently engaging and meaningful to us, captivating our attention without effort. Indeed, there is much to attend to and much to learn within the context of relating to friends and classmates. As one of our students earlier observed, our friendships are constantly transforming and challenging us in new ways. Hence, working with children's real social dilemmas can be the heart of the RLC. Much of what has occurred thus far in the curriculum is really in preparation to engaging in constructive discussion, reflection, and action within relationships that really matter to the children. "Mark's story" that began chapter 1 is one example of a real conflict that was written as a story to explore and resolve through the RLC process.

The particular relationships we focus upon in the curriculum are those that are important to children in the context of the elementary classroom—their peers and close friends. These are certainly not the only ones that could be addressed in the RLC, but are the ones that we have emphasized. In this way, the RLC can be a significant tool in the classroom community-building process. Working with real conflicts is an important way in which teachers can achieve the RLC goal of offering an avenue for examining and critiquing group norms. As teachers begin to use real conflicts occurring among the children in the classroom, discussions and role plays can help to surface tacit views and assumptions about how we want to treat one another in the classroom community. This can allow children the opportunity to more explicitly consider the kind of community they want to have in their classroom. Simultaneously, this gives teachers a vehicle for sharing the responsibility of community building with their students.

By the time the children have experienced the basic cycle of the RLC, they should have a strong working knowledge of the process. They have also begun to construct their own ideas for the meaning of the dialectic tensions. The time is ripe for both the children and the teacher to begin to reflect on how the RLC might be used to learn from real classroom dilemmas, a crucial step in helping children foster independent problem-solving strategies. Having a strong working knowledge of the basic RLC problem-solving and role play processes is important in addressing more emotionally charged and complex real dilemmas. In this way, all have a familiar procedure to guide their thought and action.

In this chapter, we offer a framework for conceptualizing the different kinds of relational conflicts that can occur among students in the elementary classroom. Within this framework, we illustrate what might be learned from different types of conflict through example conflicts that we have encountered and draw connections between these and the four dialectic tensions. We also provide guidance for teachers in thinking through which conflicts they want to address and how they want to address them (e.g., conflicts might be generally instructive to all or they might be best addressed with only the individuals in conflict).

LEVELS OF RELATIONSHIPS WITHIN
THE CLASSROOM

In working with different classrooms of children over several years, we have collected and organized the kinds of real conflicts the children have brought forward for discussion. We have noted that these conflicts can vary tremendously in complexity. Situations can also evolve and change. To help make decisions regarding which real conflicts to address and how to address them, we offer a framework that distinguishes different levels of peer relationship. Figure 6.1 contains a graphic depiction of this framework. The concentric circles represent increasingly larger groupings of individuals or layers of relationships within the classroom. Level 1 refers to an individual child, while level 2 refers to pairs of children who are close friends. Level 3 represents threesomes of children who are friends. Level 4 refers to small groups of friends, usually four to six children. Level 5 refers to the classroom community as a whole. Because many of the real conflict stories in the elementary classroom can involve one gender or the other, this last level can refer to the community of girls, the community of boys, or the classroom community as a whole.

Many of the real conflict stories that we have analyzed involved only one or two of these relational levels. For example, many stories depicted tensions between one child (level 1) and a small group (level 4). The more complex stories involving a variety of episodes over time tended to involve more of these relational levels. In the following sections, we share examples of conflict stories we have dealt with involving these different levels and discuss what might be learned from each in terms of the four dialectic tensions.

Tensions Between Individuals and Groups
(Levels 1 & 4)

Conflicts between individuals and groups can be fairly common. They typically involve a group of children struggling to play or to work with one member of the classroom. In our experience, this type of conflict is difficult for teachers to ignore.

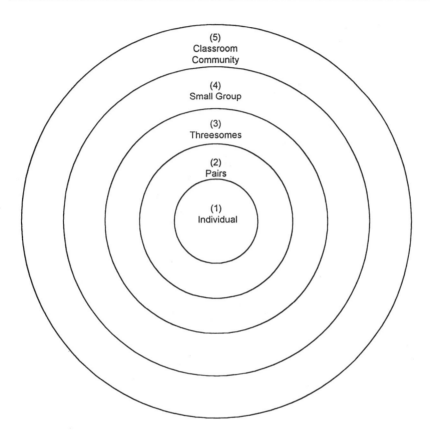

FIG. 6.1.   Levels of relationships within the classroom.

Such conflicts can lead to one child being quietly and uncom-
fortably ostracized or it can lead to disruption in various classroom group processes.

In exploring conflicts of this nature, we have observed that children can learn about the tensions between the individual and the
collective, including the challenge of balancing the needs and
rights of the individual with those of the community. Themes re-
volving around power, peer pressure, and acceptable ways of behaving have emerged in our discussions with children. Typically,
tensions of judgment and acceptance initiate the conflict, but the
independence–dependence and the expressive–protective ten-

sions have also characterized these conflicts. To further illustrate the issues that might be explored through real conflicts of this nature, we share several examples from our experience.

Explorations Into the Power of the Collective. Two example conflicts emerging from groups of second- and third-grade boys were remarkably similar in their structure and in the tensions they involved. In each case, the conflict story involved one child who felt teased by a small group during lunch. In one case, the others were taking some of the target boy's lunch, in the other story the group was verbally annoying the target boy. The initial tension seemed to be acceptance–judgment, with the group singling out or judging one boy.

As the dialogue progressed, the independence–dependence tension became evident. In acknowledging the inappropriateness of their behavior toward the target boy, the boys within one group reflected upon the dynamics of the group and the power of peer pressure. They indicated that "everybody is doing it and it is hard to stop when everybody is doing it" … "It's like you get overruled." The boys further likened the experience to a "sickness." They felt their actions were "contagious", and that the group functioned like a "virus."

The other group of boys offered some different metaphors for the same experience of group pressure. They likened it to an "addiction" and that influence or pressure was like "pushing." They also suggested the metaphor of gravity for describing the experience of group pressure, stating, "In space when you get close to a planet the atmosphere pulls you toward it … that's what's happening to Jay."

In one of these two discussions, a third tension emerged in the boys' dialogue. In addition to the group dynamic issues, these boys spent a lot of time talking about the target boy, his behavior and his character. Through their critique of him, the norms or expectations for expressive and protective aspects of communication within the group emerged. They first argued that they teased Don because "Don reacts the way we like it." They seemed to enjoy his reaction and this kept them going. As they talked further, however, they suggested Don could stop them if he changed his style of communication.

Mark:	Don gets really frustrated really fast.
Lewis:	Except he doesn't stand up for, stand up for himself.
Bob:	He doesn't stand up for himself. That's why.
Mark:	He just walks away.
Don:	It's easier when I'm not in school and I have different ways of doing that.
Mark:	OK but we're just trying to help you.
Bob:	We're just telling you, you don't stand up for yourself.

The boys went on to offer Don suggestions of how to talk to them to let them know what he needs.

The boys in both discussions clearly recognized the power of the collective over the individual. Their insights were well summed up by one boy's comments, "It is really, really hard to not do what our friends tell you." Yet, following their discussion the incidence of group teasing stopped in one situation and was greatly reduced in the other. Making the issue explicit through discussion seemed to help the boys gain some control or resistance to group influence.

Explorations Into the Power of the Individual.
Another example within this general class of conflicts came from a group of third-grade girls. In this case, a small group of girls initiated the story, expressing a good deal of concern about the behavior of one powerful girl. The girls struggled to make sense out of her motivations, defining the issue in the following comments:

We're talking about Marge getting what she wants and then letting it go.

Sometimes when something happens and we try to make up to her but she doesn't take the make-up.

The acceptance–judgment tension was evident as they discussed her character and behavior further. Their comments take on the quality of gossip apparent in other studies of talk among friends (Gottman & Parker, 1986). It has been suggested that talk of this nature actually serves a social cognitive function, helping children to sort out their own ideas and to hear the views of others regarding standards of social interaction. Some of the specific charges against Marge also hinted at violations regarding norms for instrumentality–affection within relationships:

> She (Marge) is using them ... once she gets what she wants.
>
> She's greedy ... using us.
>
> If Marge's thing doesn't happen then no one else's is going to happen.

As the girls talked, they struggled not only to understand but also to find ways to communicate with Marge. The girls understanding of the expressive–protective tension in relationships seemed central to this struggle.

Rachel: What I'm trying to say is you could say something nice—in a nice way but you can't say—Marge I don't like what you're doing. That's mean.

Teacher: How do the rest of you feel? Is that always mean? Is that always mean to tell someone you don't like what they are doing?

Susie: No.

Rachel: Well no, with Marge. With Marge it's going to be mean.

Vicky: If you say—you're not just going to say—oh, I really don't like you and walk away.

Rachel: I said, Marge I really don't like what you're doing so could we play something different today? That's like sort of mean to say that because you're sort of telling her that what she does no one likes. But you're saying it in a different tone.

Vicky: Can't you say like—Can't you say like ...

Teacher:	Couldn't you think of it as being helpful?
Rachel:	A helpful way could be, "I really like you but the things you do I don't like."
Vicky:	That's still not very well—it's like saying I really like you BUT.
Susie:	BUT is a really strong work.
Rachel:	Yea.

From the girls' exploration into how to express themselves while protecting the feelings of another, it seemed that they perceived Marge as having a unique orientation toward this tension. Their dialogue involved making their own norms for expressive and protective communication explicit and simultaneously interpreting Marge's stance in relation to these norms. In a follow-up discussion with the teacher-as-facilitator, the girls did share their feelings more directly with Marge, and this helped to improve their time together.

In reflecting on these three examples, one can see that the children explored individual differences in personality and communication styles and the power of group influence. These were extremely generative conversations, ones that clearly went beyond the limits of the initiating event. Recall that the real goal of the RLC, whether the story is real or fictional, is to move the discussion beyond the specifics of one situation to the underlying relational dynamics that may operate in many other similar situations as well. This kind of reflection is more likely to promote a deeper conceptual understanding and transfer of learning.

Changing Relationships (Levels 2, 3, & 4)

Conflicts that occur between friends in the classroom don't always come to the teacher's attention. Friends have spats or grow apart. Alliances shift. This is a necessary part of growing up. Typically, these conflicts don't greatly impact the nature of the classroom community as a whole. Although, they could, depending upon the influence of the individuals. Mostly, however, conflicts between close friends remain significant to those involved. Teachers can play an important role in supporting children's learning through their close friendships.

We share two examples, each dealing with the stability of friendships. One involved a group of three girls and the other involved a group of five boys (Fig. 6.1, levels 3 & 4, respectively). Both seemed to be essentially about changes in the relationship and the ensuing adjustments needed to maintain the balance between independence and interdependence in relating. The two discussions, however, seemed to illustrate opposite sides of the struggle.

Striving to Maintain Interdependence.   The boys' story was originally initiated by one boy who was particularly concerned that the group was "not as fun" as it used to be. As the discussion developed it was evident that others within the group had similar concerns. Some key aspects of their problem definition included:

> We're not as friendly, not getting along as well.
>
> We're not playing together as much.
>
> Used to make up games but we're not anymore ... Now only play soccer.
>
> I'm trying to have a choice, freeze tag or soccer.
>
> I'm sick of the games.
>
> Friendship not so much fun.

As the boys discussed the whys behind the problem, we noted their struggle to maintain their relationships in the face of different personal preferences. In this regard, much of the discussion centered on the games the boys liked to play and how to distribute their time equally among the different preferences. At times, it was hard to hear their concern for their friendships in all this talk about games.

> Todd: After Thursday we might play soccer, Friday we will play freeze tag, Monday we will play ...

Teacher: So that is, could the schedule be more complex than just one then the other?

Todd: Yea, it could be hard, complicated.

Carl: It's just like ... if we decide something, we just don't play those games, we just play something else.

Mark: Yea.

Jay: But sometimes, I feel like I really want to play soccer and sometimes I feel like I really want to play freeze tag. Someday it is warm, and the fields are a little muddy, cause it rained last night, and I feel sort of like, you know it is sort of like, you know it is sort of, misty outside and stuff like that. I sort of feel like I sort of want to play a little freeze tag. Once, like a really hot day, sort to want to play soccer.

Teacher: And play together ... is that the goal of the group?

Group: Yea, yea.

In a second discussion on this issue, however, we heard the boys talk more directly about their friendships. As they explored additional whys behind their problem, they argued that, "friendship is a big part of school." They further noted a challenge associated with classroom changes, "Well one thing else that is separating us, is that we are not in the same class anymore." This change seemed to increase the pressure they felt for finding quality recess time together.

Jay: If we keep, if Mark and me and if Todd, Mark, and me, if Todd and me keep playing freeze tag and Todd keeps playing soccer, and we are not playing together anymore ... we are going to shift level.

Teacher: Shift level? ... Maybe drift apart?

Jay: Mark is going to drift apart in his sport world. We are going to drift apart into tag games and stuff.

Clearly the boys worried about the friendship, not playing regularly together, and drifting apart. They were beginning to see the effects of different points of view and different preferences for the stability of their relationships. They really wanted to get these concerns aired and share their commitment to their relationships. They all wanted to find a way to play together while honoring their independent interests. To resolve their problem and tip the balance back toward greater interdependence, they decided on a schedule of games. They set aside two days for playing what each individual might want to play and three days where they all have to come back together to play. They felt their solution of monitoring and maintaining time together was going to address their worries, as noted by one boy, "so then we come back together so we can't lose our friendship."

Searching for Independence. A girls' story of relational change began with a focus on their difficulty with direct and clear communication. The initiating event in their story was an incident where one member of the threesome was pinched and teased by the other two. The girls expressed a difficulty in sharing their feelings and needs with one another in clear ways that also preserved their relationship (expressive–protective tension). Erin acknowledged how difficult it was for her to say what she needed in several comments.

Hannah: Well see I usually never said it. But yesterday I said it but I didn't really say. I was like soft. I don't like—

Susie–
Vicky: I didn't hear you.

Hannah: I didn't say it loud. That's what I'm trying to say … I said stop and I couldn't even hear myself.

Teacher: It was loud on the bus?

Hannah: No it wasn't that, I didn't want to say it. I didn't want to say stop.

Teacher: So is that part of the problem?

Susie: She didn't find her strength.

Hannah: I usually don't find my strength.

When they don't "find their strength" to share their feelings, the girls admitted that their problems usually escalated. Their discussion further suggested that they may not fully know their own feelings and needs. They seemed to be all mixed up in the other. When they felt the need to articulate the boundaries between self and other, they also feared losing the friendship. The intensity of their connection suggested a struggle in achieving independence within their relationship.

Susie: Every time any of us gets unhappy we really care for each other and we really like each other and we always think that the person who is sad is mad at the other two people because ... I don't know.

Vicky: She won't talk to us then.

Susie: We always feel guilty ... If I'm sad I hardly ever talk to them because I don't want to talk about what happened...we never really find our strength to tell each other what is going on.

Hannah: Cause it's mean. You know some things are sort of private.

These two examples offer glimpses into the experiences of children as their friendships shift and change. They also suggest the kinds of insights children may gain by taking time to reflect. The root of these changes seemed well characterized by the challenge of maintaining the delicate balance between independence and dependence in communication and action. The boys' efforts seemed directed at maintaining an interdependence that they felt was being threatened. In this regard, they identified time together as key. The girls' efforts seemed more directed at arriving at independent stances toward problematic events. In this respect, they articulated the need for each to find their own individual strength to feel and to communicate clearly with one another when difficulties arose. In their dialogue, the girls also seemed to be examining the tacit norms for expressive–protective communication within their relationship and suggesting some needed changes in order for each individual to grow.

Although these friendship challenges and explorations may not always be central to the academic agenda of the classroom teacher, one can see how periodic attention to these may be fruitful. When children's close friendships are threatened and unbalanced, they may be highly distracted and unproductive in class. When they have a brief opportunity over a lunch period or two to disclose some of their concerns and to make a plan for action, they may function better within the classroom. Moreover, the teacher gains access to their thoughts, feelings, and perspectives on various issues. What they learn may be helpful in planning various group activities and making recommendations regarding future class placements.

Changing Relationships Within the Community (Levels 2 & 5)

Changing relationships can sometimes occur on a larger scale, involving many different episodes and several dyads and triads of friends in the classroom. These conflicts can be more disruptive to the classroom than those just explored. They may also be quite complex for the teacher and the participants to explore. We offer two illustrations. The first is fairly well defined and leads to a clarification in classroom social roles. The second is a bit more ambiguous and less conclusive. We offer each example to clarify what might be gained, and the risks in addressing complex social issues.

Exploring the Nature of Group Divisions. Examining real conflicts within the classroom community can reveal hidden divisions and actually break down certain myths about groups. One such example involved the community of girls within the classroom. This discussion was initiated by a girl who was feeling excluded by the girls in the class. She defined the problem as the "majority excluding the minority." She clearly articulated the story as one involving the acceptance and judgment tension in her following comments:

Two groups are repelling each other.

Majority is excluding the minority from practically everything just because they have different personalities.

We're different and so the majority is persecuting the minority.

I'm feeling excluded from the class. It doesn't have a single
thing to do with recess ... it doesn't have anything to do with
playing. It has to do with conversation and relationships.

A good deal of the discussion centered on the meaning of the
terms "majority" and "minority," and their validity for describing the classroom dynamics. In the discussion, equal numbers
of girls identified themselves as feeling part of the minority and
as those feeling part of the majority. Interestingly, they retained
the use of the majority–minority language to describe the problem despite the fact that the literal meaning involving number
really did not apply.

As they defined and explored the problem, several issues were
raised. These included: personality difference ("birds of a
feather flock together," "they're a million miles away," "one of the
majority is different from the other majority ... everybody is different"), a lack of knowledge of the other's mind ("the majority
didn't know how the minority felt"), a lack of communication
("minority doesn't speak up"), and the history of friendships and
classroom placements ("the minority had friends in first grade,
now they're in a different class").

In their continued use of minority and majority, the girls implicitly recognized the power dynamics in the classroom.
Clearly there were some who felt disenfranchised from the
mainstream, lacking in social benefits (i.e., "conversation and
relationships"). The group struggled with how to address these
feelings. In their role-played resolutions, they emphasized a
lack of knowledge and faulty communication as the root causes.
In so doing, they seemed to attribute greater power to the minority than this group originally believed they had.

The dialogue that occurred among these girls cleared the air.
There was a sense of relief in sharing these feelings. It also became evident to many that they weren't so alone in feeling they

were the minority. These girls felt listened to, and as a result, more empowered through the dialogue. Others expressed a greater sensitivity to the experience of the girls they typically don't play with in the classroom, and seemed to feel greater respect for them as well.

Taking Sides.   One situation we encountered illustrated how a problem can mushroom. What initially seemed to be a problem between two friends actually became many problems between different friends within the community of girls. As the girls discussed the situation, they began to recognize the complexities of group dynamics. "Taking sides" was a metaphor the girls used again and again to describe their experience in the group. They saw it as easier when they were just with one other friend. With more players, it got difficult. They concluded that the real problem was "all the different relationships" and their struggle to manage them.

Sandy:	I think it is true for everyone because it's hard to decide who to be with, then they take sides when there are more people.
Ann:	Right, I think it is the same for all of us. With only two people you can't take sides.
Sandy:	You can't take sides.
Teacher:	What is taking sides about when you are together?
Sandy:	It is sort of like someone likes someone and someone doesn't, that is sort of like that.
Teacher:	People are trying to influence one another.

The group seemed to highlight the acceptance–judgment tension as they introduced the notion of taking sides. Yet, when they discussed the influences of close relationships on these judgments, the independence–dependence struggle became evident. The girls felt influenced by others and compelled to display certain alliances with others who in turn had effects on other relationships within the group. The girls concluded that it worked "best when we're only two people." They also acknowledged the need to "take your own side" and to "remember how you feel."

One girl offered some wonderful insights into how she experienced friendship from one year to the next:

> I don't know my friends from last year as well, so I feel like I don't have any friends. And I am lonely and I don't make friends as easily when I get older, it is kind of harder ... Like kindergarten everyone was always playing and it was easy and the more work you do the harder it is to make friends. You can't talk as much ... And people's feelings can get hurt more often when you get older ... We were really good friends in first grade, now we're making new friends ... It is like every year someone new comes in ... so every year our friendship changes.

This child's comments in many respects reflected the developmental literature's account of change in children's friendships from early to middle childhood. With a greater degree of interdependence between friends comes greater challenge and responsibility. This child's account offered an additional insight, however. That is, the experience of friendships within the context of groups. She indicated that changes in the structure of their school day (i.e., more work and less play) and changes in the composition of the classrooms also brought change in the experience of the friendship relationships within the group. Such change would seem to further complicate the management of the various tensions inherent in close relationships. It could also pose challenges in the management of classroom groups for teachers.

Within both of these examples, the children had an opportunity to step back from the complex interactions taking place between various individuals to reflect upon patterns in those interactions. In the first example, the girls became aware of the feelings of the quieter girls for the first time. There was some discomfort with the charges of the minority individuals and the dynamics they exposed. At the same time, the dialogue dispelled some assumptions the minority group made and seemed to bring all closer together. The open yet structured communication afforded by the RLC made it easier for these girls to confront sensitive issues of inclusion within the classroom and arrive at a healthier sense of community. The second example was one that never was really resolved because it was not about one problem. Many small tensions existed among the girls. What they did achieve, however, was a clearer awareness of this and the fact that they responded by taking sides.

CHOOSING PROBLEMS TO ADDRESS

In the examples we explored, one can see that there are valuable lessons to be learned through conflicts involving the various levels of relationship within the classroom. Many of these conflicts can be simultaneously occurring within a classroom community, so not all can be addressed. For this reason, it is important for teachers to reflect and determine the social issues they see as most important to their students' growth. They also need to consider which relationships within the classroom seem most in need of guidance and support. These two factors are helpful in developing criteria for choosing spontaneous classroom dilemmas to explore and resolve through the RLC. Clearly, there is not enough time in a classroom to respond to each problem that occurs and not every problem deserves the attention afforded it through the process.

The following are questions to consider in making decisions about the problems you choose to address through the RLC. They take into account the participants, the potential issues, and the teacher's point of view.

- Is the conflict drawing too much attention away from normal classroom learning processes?
- How many individuals does it involve?
- How significant is the conflict to the individuals involved?
- How significant is the conflict to the healthy functioning of the community?

- Is a child or children suffering greatly as a result of this conflict?

- What kind of issues might come up if the conflict is explored?

- Which issues do I think are most important to my students' growth?

- Which issues am I most comfortable in addressing?

- What are my own beliefs and biases on the potential issues? How clear are they to me?

- Have other similar conflicts been occurring?

- What are the wishes and interests of the children's parents?

- Are my students and I comfortable and confident with the process?

Many factors can enter into the decision to work with a real conflict. Obviously, when it involves many children or is taking time and attention away from learning, it has to be addressed. Some problems are common occurrences for all the children and probing the issues as a group may prevent, minimize, or help children negotiate them more constructively in future occurrences. For example, the problem of negotiating activities for limited recess time is a conflict that may resonate with many of the children. In the event that a child or a group of children are being systematically excluded and feel hurt by this, the RLC can offer a supportive process. As you prepare to address any conflict, however, it would be important to consider the kinds of related issues that might arise. For example, we have seen issues of peer pressure, inclusion–exclusion, personality differences, communication style differences, personal biases, and racism surface through discussion. One's own comfort level, as well as the children's, in exploring such issues is important to assess. Taking time to reflect upon the aforementioned questions may allow you to develop a clear set of criteria for where you want to go in using the children's own conflict in the RLC. It is important to have a firm sense of your purpose and a high comfort level with the process.

WHO NEEDS TO BE INVOLVED?

Determining the individuals to involve in the discussion is a second decision point in working with real conflicts. Several questions are helpful in making this determination. Carefully thinking these through is important before moving forward.

- Who is involved in the conflict?
- Who could benefit by participating in the RLC process?
- What are the confidentiality concerns?

Typically it is best to involve only those in the conflict. In this way, they can deal directly with each other and determine what they want to change. We conducted most of the examples previously described in this way. At times, individuals come forward to complain about another individual. It may be helpful to have them write a story and require that all be present to explore the issues. In this way, the group is not talking behind anyone's back. In one previous example, the girls did start with a meeting without the girl they had concerns about. A follow-up meeting was held, however, in which this girl was included. In this case, the initial meeting seemed important in helping the girls to clarify their feelings and articulate their goals for communicating with the other girl.

As previously noted some conflicts can be representative of many others that have occurred (or are likely to occur) in the classroom and the whole class may actually benefit from discussing the issues. In this event, having the initiating students compose a story that depicts the conflict but retains the anonymity of those involved can be a good way to begin. With the permission of the authors, the story can then be read to the whole class for the discussion and role-play process.

Finally, there are situations that clearly involve the whole class and they know it. For example, we witnessed a RLC meeting concerning a classroom communities' dilemma of interacting with and including a new non-English speaking student. In this event, the teacher composed the story for discussion so as to maximize the number of individuals who appreciate the dilemma. One or two students could also compose the story. This was the case in the previous dilemma highlighting the majority–minority division within the class.

Confidentiality is a consideration when individuals begin to share their own feelings and experiences. The students should agree to and be assured that what they say will stay within the group. At the same time, however, if a conflict promises to be highly personal in nature or to raise overly controversial issues, it may not be most appropriately dealt with through the RLC. Highly sensitive conflicts may be best handled through the mental health personnel (social worker, school psychologist, counselor) in the school or in conjunction to his or her services. Commonly occurring conflicts, dilemmas involving typical social developmental concerns, and problems distracting to the functioning of the classroom community are usually good candidates for the RLC process.

VARIATIONS IN THE RLC PROCESS WITH REAL CONFLICT

Using the RLC process with real conflict is much the same as described in the previous chapters with some modification. In the case of actual conflicts, the child or children initiating the concern and request for the discussion typically write the story. At times this can have parent involvement as in our example in chapter 1. The teacher acts as facilitator using the three main problem-solving questions as in any RLC discussion, however, for the "why is this happening?" question, a new emphasis is taken. At this point, it is important to probe for each child's point of view, so this segment of the discussion surfaces all perspectives on the conflict. In this way, the children come to know how all the others involved are thinking and feeling. Choices can be handled in a similar manner. Usually specific choices for each of the individuals involved can be identified. The group may wish to try them out immediately through a role play, but often times we have found this to be less necessary with real conflict. The choices often involve trying something out at recess the next day or modifying how one is thinking about a situation. In such cases, the group can commit to change by setting some reasonable goals related to the various choices. For example, the boys in one of the conflicts we previously described each agreed to treat each other differently during their lunch period.

Although true for all RLC sessions, the most important characteristic of the RLC with real conflict is the children's ownership of the process. It works best when they are already familiar enough with the steps of the discussion process to need no real support with it. The teacher needs to facilitate and allow the children to voice their positions. He or she needs to let them identify what they believe are the most viable ways to resolve the situation. Certainly there can be conflicts that are not resolvable in a half-hour meeting. We have held additional sessions because we needed to continue to clarify the problem or to follow up on the choices to see how they worked out in reality. The teacher's role is to make sure the issues have been understood and thoroughly explored by those involved and that some constructive direction for the resolution has been achieved. At some point, depending on the conflict, the teacher may need to help shape the direction of the discussion by clarifying school rules or other agreed upon guidelines for behavior.

CONCLUSIONS

The RLC has a great deal of utility with a variety of typical social problems arising within the culture of the elementary school classroom. It provides a supportive and flexible structure for all to clarify perspectives and to define a course of action. Through the process, the children have a great deal of ownership, taking responsibility for exploring and changing their behavior in relationship to their classmates.

We suggested distinguishing the children's conflicts on the basis of the different levels of relationship they involve. In doing so, a teacher may begin to systematically anticipate the kinds of issues that may be explored through the process and the players who need to be involved. In addition to these levels and the kinds of issues that surface from conflicts involving each, we noted several important questions to guide teacher decision making. It may be useful to reflect over this framework and set of questions at the start of the school year and to revisit it periodically as your knowledge of the children and the group dynamics grow. In this way, a teacher may make informed and thoughtful decisions about which social dilemmas he or she wishes to address.

7

Making It Your Own: Professional Development and the Relational Literacy Curriculum

"Take charge of your own mind ..."

INTRODUCTION

In the preceding chapters, we have presented the groundwork for implementing the RLC. Specifically, we outlined a set of procedures for implementing story–problem discussions, role plays, and group reflections. In addition to procedures, we have provided action frameworks to guide teacher decision making. These frameworks, we believe, are essential to the curriculum's success because they allow for teacher's to build upon theory while integrating their own procedures in meaningful ways. Thus, teachers can make use of the RLC according to their own needs. It is a means by which teachers can address educational social issues pertinent to their contexts, while enriching their own professional development.

In this chapter, we review the four action-oriented frameworks that organize implementation of each aspect of the curriculum (i.e., the story discussion, the role plays, the reflection across stories, and the use of real conflict), summarizing the essential principles associated with each. We draw implications for teachers' learning and professional growth.

THE ACTION FRAMEWORKS OF THE RLC

The action frameworks presented within chapters 3 through 6 are intended to guide the way in which we view and understand the action within the RLC. They are intended to support thinking about the action and facilitate decision making about what to do next. They also help to keep in mind the individual as well as the social-learning processes discussed in chapter 2 in relation to the four goals of the RLC. The frameworks directly relate to much of the theory and research discussed in chapter 2, but they are more specific to the action of one aspect of the curriculum or another.

Chapter 3 presented a way of viewing the explanations of conflict that children provide. We noted that explanations focus on one character, the circumstances, the difference between two characters, their interactions, or their relationship as a whole. We suggested that these different explanation types vary in terms of the amount of information being taken into account, with those focusing on the interactions or the relationship being more developmentally sophisticated than those focusing only on one character's perspective. This framework provided a way to listen to children's explanations about relational conflict and a direction in which to encourage children's thinking.

We also emphasized the four dialectic tensions as a way of characterizing conflict within a story. The dialectic tensions of judgment–acceptance, independence–dependence, expressive–protective, and instrumentality–affection focus our attention on the dynamics between the characters. In learning about these tensions, we hope to encourage children to focus on conflict in more relational ways, that is, in terms of the perspectives of all characters within the relationship and their interactions over time.

Putting the continuum of explanations together with the four dialectic tensions, we have a way of monitoring children's ac-

tion and understanding of relationships through the curriculum. Appendix B provides a Discussion Framework that
summarizes these dimensions. This framework highlights the
internal learning processes from a developmental and a contextual perspective. The range of explanation types represents
developmentally more complex ways of thinking and explaining social conflict. The four tensions represent different relational contexts that children may experience and reflect upon.
This framework could be used to summarize the frequency of
various kinds of explanations offered by the children in discussing the different tension stories. We provide additional
tools and rubrics for teachers to use to monitor their own
prompts and the children's explanations over time. Teachers
may wish to use these to anticipate problem-solving discussions and to reflect on the nature of the children's understanding of relationships and social conflict. They provide a quick
reference on how to listen as the discussion unfolds and how to
summarize what happened.

Chapter 4 provides a developmental framework for characterizing the children's learning through the role play aspect of
the RLC. This framework also highlights the importance of perspective taking, however, the focus is less on how the children
are reflecting upon the perspectives and the tensions. Rather, it
emphasizes how they can represent them through action. Role
taking is the least sophisticated way of enacting a character's
perspective. Children in this phase need time to rehearse or to
script their performance. The emphasis of this phase revolves
around building dialogue skills, reducing performance anxiety,
modeling audience expectations, and strengthening relational
understanding through discussion following the action. Role
playing is a more sophisticated phase, where children need only
minimal prompts to help them enact a role. The emphasis in
this phase is on the conflict rather than the resolution, representing the tension within the conflict, and working toward
greater spontaneity and creativity. Role creating is the most sophisticated phase of learning through enactment. Role creators
are facile at enacting a role with little scripting or support, spontaneously improvising in response to other players. The emphasis here is on encouraging more truthful personal enactments.

The role play framework offers a guide for viewing the children's role plays. It highlights both internal and social-learning processes, helping teachers to make decisions about role play partners and how much support they will need. Appendix C provides a graphic depiction of the role play developmental framework, followed by additional tools and worksheets that can aid teachers in implementing the role plays. We provide a summary of the discussion questions to use following role plays and worksheets for students to use as they plan their role plays.

Chapter 5 provides guidance for the sessions in which the children reflect across different stories they have discussed and role played. This occurs once they have had stories involving each of the four tensions. The purpose of this reflection is to introduce the dialectic tension concepts to the children so they can begin to use these concepts more explicitly to understand relationships and conflict in their lives. We share a framework linking the children's own language to the stories that have been discussed to the relevant tension terms to help teachers accomplish this purpose. This Connections Framework defines the essential process that we have found most useful in introducing the concept of the dialectic tensions to children. There are alternative ways in which this may be accomplished, and we discuss several examples of these in the chapter. Others that teachers develop using the Connections Framework may be equally helpful.

The Connections Framework highlights the important constructivist learning process involving making connections between familiar terms and knowledge and the new concept of the dialectic tensions. Once again, we graphically depict the Connections Framework in Appendix D. Two reference tools for the specific ways in which we have accomplished reflection across the stories and the introduction of the tension terms are also provided. These appendices are intended as a quick reference. The framework can also serve as a vehicle for designing additional procedures.

Chapter 6 explores the use of children's real conflict within the RLC. We provide a framework for distinguishing different kinds of peer relationship configurations typically occurring among elementary age students, including friendship dyads, threesomes, small groups, and the community as a whole. The Levels of Relationship Framework is intended to help teachers organize the social context of the classroom. It provides a simple means to differentiate the actual conflicts and to help make decisions regarding which conflicts to address through the RLC. Conflicts involving many levels may be overly complex, while those involving single levels may be less so. Also certain relationship levels tend to surface particular issues and tensions. We illustrated some of these possibilities through the example conflict discussions that we shared. Appendix E offers a graphic depiction of the Levels of Relationship Framework along with steps and questions to guide decision making on real conflicts, and includes reflection questions to aid teacher decision making.

THE ACTION FRAMEWORKS
AND TEACHER LEARNING

Together the action frameworks reflect the four goals of the curriculum, highlighting the individual and social learning that can take place through the RLC. In concert, they set up a powerful learning environment in which children practice perspective taking through reflection and action, make conceptual connections between the novel and the familiar, and apply conceptual connections in the context of real conflicts. These same opportunities go a long way in promoting group cohesion and group identity. Children evolve a shared language that allows them to discuss difficult issues. They also have an opportunity to more explicitly examine their values and assumptions about relating. Thus, they are in a better position to make conscious decisions about important ways of behaving within their classroom community.

The frameworks provide benefits to teachers as well. They are designed to allow teachers freedom in implementing the curriculum by establishing a guide without too narrowly prescribing a teacher's actions. In this way, teachers may explore and support the social world of their classroom with a sense of purpose, and at the same time, adapt what they are doing to what they see and experience with their students. The action frameworks can actually help teachers to learn about the peer culture in their classroom, the uniqueness of the children and their peer relationships. They provide a lens through which to organize their observations as well as their actions.

As teachers' familiarity and comfort with the action frameworks grow, their engagement with students in the RLC can be richer and more complex. Teachers tend to notice more and to incorporate these new observations into their teaching. New actions then provide new opportunities to see and learn even more. The use of the tools within the appendix can support this cycle of reflection and action. They provide a systematic way of recording important events within the RLC and monitoring changes over time in both the students' and the teacher's performance. Working in this way can be an important source of continuing professional development.

REVISITING THE VALUES AND COMMITMENTS OF THE RLC

In thinking further about teacher professional growth through the RLC, we reflected upon our own learning over the past seven years as we developed this curriculum. In doing so, we revisited our initial values and commitments with respect to working with children:

- Relationships are an important domain of study.
- Children have competence from which adults can learn.
- Dialogue is an important way to learn.
- A sense of community is important to learning.

We recognized that these values apply equally to our own professional learning as they did for the students we served. We saw that it was important to consider and to invest time in our professional relationships as we worked. The more explicitly we as professionals understood our working relationship, the more effectively we worked together. As we shared our observations of children's views and struggles with the dialectic tensions with other professionals, parallels between the children's accounts and those of adults were frequently evident. We heard echoes of our own puzzlements, and frequently reaffirmed the importance of listening to the wisdom of children. We also appreciated again and again the importance of engaging children early in discourse that allowed for the exploration of peer relationships. By learning and practicing a relational way of thinking during the elementary years, we believe individuals will have a stronger foundation for constructively engaging with others as they grow into adolescence and adulthood.

Widening our circle of dialogue to include a variety of colleagues has also been valuable in implementing the RLC. In one instance, we collaborated with all the third-grade teachers in one building, and in doing so, built a broader understanding of the social dynamics within a third- grade community of students. We shared stories, and at times, wrote stories together that helped to address the issues we saw. In discussing our experience, we all gained new insights into how to more effectively engage in the RLC. In other instances, we implemented the curriculum with teachers responsible for different grade levels in a building. Through these dialogues we began to understand the real power of a developmental perspective. We deepened our understanding of the dialectic tensions and how children engaged with these concepts over time. We saw great value in having children cycle through these concepts over two years in order to deepen their understanding of the dynamics of relating and how to change patterns as conflict arose.

In using a collaborative approach to the RLC across classrooms and grade levels the potential for community building is greatly enhanced. All the shared benefits referred to for a classroom can evolve for a larger community. Shared language, stories, and frameworks operate as resources across classrooms for teachers and students. In this way, all members of the larger community have some say in articulating the norms of acceptable behavior. Moreover, there are shared ways of responding when conflicts develop that focus on learning and shared responsibility rather than punishment and blame. Perhaps most importantly, the use of the RLC within several classrooms offers shared opportunities for teachers to connect not only around issues of learning and curriculum, but also around relationships.

Teachers gain insights together about the dynamics of groups and how best to support the continued growth and development of everyone.

REVISITING THE MEANING OF RELATIONAL LITERACY

At the start of this volume, we defined relational literacy as the ability to reflect upon and to negotiate relationships in personally meaningful ways. Throughout this volume, we provide frameworks to capture the dynamics of relating as well as to scaffold the teaching-learning process. A broad conceptual framework based upon the learning goals of the RLC offers a theoretical foundation. Four action frameworks that more specifically organize the implementation of its major components offer a practical foundation. Stories and example discussions are woven throughout the volume to illustrate how the RLC can work. These illustrations, however, are not the only way it can work. Through careful listening, dialogue, reflection, and planning, teachers can tailor the curriculum to best meet their students' needs. We believe the RLC works best in this way. When teachers work closely with their students to learn about relationships through the various RLC frameworks, they can make the curriculum their own.

References

Adalbjarnardottir, S. (1992). Fostering children's social conflict resolutions in the classroom: A developmental approach. In F. K. Oser, A. Dick, & J. L. Patry (Eds.), *Effective & responsible teaching: The new synthesis.* San Francisco: Jossey-Bass.

Argyris, C., & Schon, D. (1974). *Theory and practice: Increasing professional effectiveness.* San Francisco: Jossey-Bass.

Bakhtin, M. M. (1981). *The dialogic imagination: Four essays by M. M. Bakhtin* (M. Holquist, Ed.; E. Emerson & M. Holquist, Trans.). Austin: University of Texas Press.

Baxter, L., & Montgomery, B. (1996). *Relating: Dialogue and dialectics.* New York: Guilford.

Blatner, A. (1988). *Foundations of psychodrama: History, theory and practice.* New York: Springer.

Bruner, J. (1990). *Acts of meaning.* Cambridge, MA: Harvard University Press.

Caplan, M., Weissberg, R. P., Gorber, J. S., Sivo, P. J., Grady, K., & Jacoby, C. (1992). Social competence promotion with inner-city and suburban young adolescents: Effects on social adjustment and alcohol use. *Journal of Consulting and Clinical Psychology, 60,* 56–63.

Cantor, N., & Kihlstrom, J. F. (1987). *Personality and social intelligence.* Englewood Cliffs, NJ: Prentice Hall.

Chi, M. T., Feltovich, P. J., & Glaser, R. (1981). Categorization and representation of physics problems by experts and novices. *Cognitive Science, 5,* 121–152.

Chiodo, J. J., & Klausmeier, R. L. (1984). "V. T."—the extra step in classroom role playing. *The Social Studies, 75*(3), 122–123.

Corsaro, W. (1985). *Friendship and the peer culture in the early years.* Norwood, NJ: Ablex Publishing.

Courtney, R. (1990). *Drama and intelligence: A cognitive theory.* Montreal, Canada: McGill-Queen's University Press.

Damon, W. (1977). *The social world of the child.* San Francisco: Jossey-Bass.

Duck, S., Miell, D. K., & Gaebler, H. C. (1980). Attraction and communication in children's interactions. In H. C. Foot, A. J. Chapman, & J. R. Smith (Eds.), *Friendship and social relations in children* (pp. 89–115). New York: Wiley.

Dweck, C. S., & Leggett, E. L. (1988). A social-cognitive approach to motivation and personality. *Psychological Review, 95,* 256–273.

Ericsson, K. A., & Smith, J. (1991). *Toward a general theory of expertise.* New York: Cambridge University Press.

Gardner, H. (1983). *Frames of mind: The theory of multiple intelligences.* New York: Basic Books.

Gergen, K. J. (1994). *Realities and relationships.* Cambridge, MA: Harvard University Press.

Gettinger, M., Doll, B., & Salmon, D. (1994). Effects of social problem-solving, goal-setting, and parent training on children's peer relationships. *Journal of Applied Developmental Psychology, 15,* 141–163.

Gottman, J. M., & Mettetal, G. (1986). Speculation about social and affective development: Friendship and acquaintanceship through adolescence. In J. M. Gottman & J. G. Parker (Eds.), *Conversations of friends* (pp. 192–237). New York: Cambridge University Press.

Gottman, J. M., & Parker, J. G. (1986). *Conversations of friends.* New York: Cambridge University Press.

Heider, F. (1958). *The psychology of interpersonal relationships.* New York: Wiley.

Hyerle, D. (1996). *Visual tools for constructing knowledge.* Alexandra, VA: Association for Supervision and Curriculum Development.

Johnson, D. R. (1982). Developmental approaches in drama therapy. *The Arts in Psychotherapy, 9,* 183–189.

Kelly, G. (1955). *The psychology of personal constructs.* New York: Norton.

Klein, S. (1999). *Analysis of children's perceptions of the Relational Literacy Curriculum.* Unpublished master's thesis, National-Louis University, Evanston, IL.

Kolodner, J. (1997). Educational implications of analogy. A view of case-based reasoning. *American Psychologist, 52,* 57–66.

Lakoff, G. (1993). The contemporary theory of metaphor. In A. Ortony (Ed.), *Metaphor and thought* (pp. 202–251). New York: Cambridge University Press.

Lakoff, G., & Johnson, M. (1980). *Metaphors we live by.* Chicago: University of Chicago Press.

Moreno, J. L. (1953). *Who shall survive?* Roanoke, VA: Royal Publishing Company.

Ortony, A. (1993) *Metaphor and thought* (2nd ed.). New York: Cambridge University Press.

Pelligrini, D. S., & Urban, E. S. (1985). An evaluation of interpersonal cognitive problem solving training with children. *Journal of Child Psychology and Psychiatry, 26,* 17–41.

Rawlins, W. K. (1992). *Friendship matters.* New York: Aldine De Gruyter.

Rogoff, B. (1990). *Apprenticeship in thinking.* New York: Oxford University Press.

Salmon, D., & Fenning. P. (1993). A process of mentorship in school consultation. *Journal of Educational and Psychological Consultation, 4,* 69–87.

Salmon, D., & Freedman, R. A. (1995). *Anticipating friendship: Views from the classroom.* Paper presented at the annual meeting of the American Educational Research Association, San Francisco.

Salmon, D. & Freedman, R. A. (1997). *Every year our friendship changes.* Paper presented at the annual meeting of the American Educational Research Association, Chicago.

Salmon, D. & Freedman, R. A. (1998). *The social construction of friendship.* Paper presented at the annual meeting of the American Educational Research Association, San Diego, CA.

Salmon, D., & Freedman, R. A. (1999). *Collaboration on relational literacy.* Chicago: Spencer Foundation Small Grants Report.

Salmon, D., & Freedman, R. A. (2000). *Children's relational concepts in the context of a relational literacy curriculum.* Paper presented at the annual meeting of the American Educational Research Association, New Orleans, LA.

Sandberg, B. (1981). A descriptive scale for drama, In G. Schattner & R. Courtney (Eds.), *Drama in therapy* (Vol. 1, pp. 29–55). New York: Drama Book Specialists.

Schon, D. A. (1993). Generative metaphor: A perspective on problem-setting in social policy. In A. Ortony (Ed.), Metaphor *and thought* (2nd ed., pp.137–163). New York: Cambridge University Press.

Selman, R. L. (1980). *The growth of interpersonal understanding: Developmental and clinical analyses.* New York: Academic Press.

Selman, R. L., & Schultz, L. H. (1990). *Making a friend in youth.* Chicago: University of Chicago Press.

Selman, R. L., Watts, C. L., & Schultz, L. H. (1997). *Fostering friendship. Pair therapy for treatment and prevention.* New York: Aldine De Gruyter.

Stanford, G. (1974). Why role playing fails. *English Journal, 63,* 54.

Sternberg, P., & Garcia, A. (1989). *Sociodrama: Who's in your shoes.* New York: Praeger.

Sullivan, H. S. (1953). *The interpersonal theory of psychiatry.* New York: Norton.

van Ments, M. (1983). *The effective use of role play: A handbook for teachers and trainers.* London: Kogan Page Ltd.

Voss, J. F., Greene, T. R., Post, T. A., & Penner, B. C. (1983). Problem-solving skills in social sciences In G.H. Bower (Ed.), *The psychology of learning and memory* (pp. 165–213). New York: Academic Press.

Voss, J. F., Sherman, W., Tyler, S. W., & Yengo, L. A. (1983). Individual differences in the solving of social science problems. In R. F. Dillon & R. R. Schmeck (Eds.), *Individual differences in cognition,* (pp 205–232). New York: Academic Press.

Vygotsky, L. V. (1978). *Mind in society: The development of higher psychological processes.* Cambridge, MA: Harvard University Press.

Wells, G. (1989). Language in the classroom: Literacy and collaborative talk. *Language and Education, 3,* 251–273.

Wright, L. (1984). A theory of instruction. *Children's Theatre Review, 33*(2), 18.

Youniss, J. (1980). *Parents and peers in social development. A Sullivan-Piaget perspective.* Chicago: University of Chicago Press.

Table of Contents
for Appendixes

Appendix A

- Timeline for the Relational Literacy Curriculum

Appendix B

- Discussion Framework
- Conceptual Scheme: Rawlins Dialectic Tensions
- Sample Stories by Tension
- Template for Group-Recording Notes
- Quality Discussion Rubric
- Quality of Child Explanations—Definitions
- Quality of Child Explanations—Rubric
- Discussion Reflection Tool
- Teacher Prompts—Definitions
- Teacher Prompts—Matrix
- Conceptual Prompts by Tension

Appendix C

- Role Playing Framework
- Role Play: Questions for Guidance
- Role Play Worksheet

Appendix D

- Conceptual Connections Framework
- Story-Sort Chart
- Circle Maps
  - Judgment–Acceptance
  - Independence–Dependence
  - Expressive–Protective
  - Instrumentality–Affection

Appendix E

- Levels of Relationship Framework
- Steps in Solving Real Conflicts

Appendix A
Timeline for the Relational Literacy Curriculum

TIMELINE FOR THE RLC

Basic Cycle	September—December
Week One:	1st Story–Discussion—Judgement–Acceptance
Week Two:	Role Play
Week Three:	2nd Story–Discussion—Independence–Dependence
Week Four:	Role Play
Week Five:	3rd Story–Discussion—Expressive–Protective
Week Six:	Role Play
Week Seven:	4th Story– Discussion—Instrumentality–Affection
Week Eight:	Role Play
Week Nine:	Tension Discussion

Sources:

- Details about the basic discussion are included in chapter 3.
- Details about the role play are included in chapter 4.
- Details about the tension discussion are included in chapter 5.

Contextualizing Cycle   January—June

- Children Write Stories   – 1 week
- Discussion–Role Plays Continues in Two-Week Cycle
  - Week 1—Discussion
  - Week 2—Role play
- Children's Real Conflicts Emerge—
  {May substitute for stories}
- Metaphor Mapping—(if emerge)

Sources:

- Details about children writing stories are in chapter 5.
- Details about Real Conflicts are in chapter 6.
- Details about Metaphors in chapter 5.

Appendix B
The Discussion Process

TABLE B.1
Discussion Framework

Relational Tensions	Judgment–Acceptance	Independence–Dependence	Expressive–Protective	Instrumentality–Affection
Child Explanations	Criteria for Judging Friendship	Nature of Healthy Interdependency in Friendship	Emotional Mechanisms in Communication	Constraints on Relationships
Character Interpretation				
Character Differences				
Character Interactions				
Character Relationship				
Metaphors or Personal Stories				
Character Circumstance				

TABLE B.2
Conceptual Scheme: Rawlins Dialectic Tensions

Independence–Dependence	Tension between feeling free to pursue one's own interests and remaining available to the other to sustain the relationship.
Expressive–Protective	Tension between communicating one's feelings and needs, and strategically protecting oneself or the feelings of the other.
Judgment–Acceptance	Tension between evaluating and holding the friend to some standards versus largely accepting the friend for who he or she is.
Instrumentality–Affection	Tension between valuing another as a means to an end versus valuing another as an end in itself.

SAMPLE STORIES BY TENSION

Judgment–Acceptance Stories

It was the start of another new school year. But this year Jamie was feeling anxious because her best friend was not going to be in her room anymore. In fact, her friend was not even coming back to the same school. Jamie was worried about who she was going to eat with and play with. It seemed like everything was going to be different this year, and she wasn't sure if she was going to like it.

Almost all the third-grade boys liked to play together on the playground. The group had known each other since kindergarten and they really got along well. Except there was one boy who didn't get included—Paul. Most of the others really didn't enjoy him very much. They usually avoided him at recess and lunch, made jokes behind his back, and even teased him right to his face. Neil, one of the group members began to feel bad about what was happening to Paul. He thought about how he would feel if he were Paul. He wondered what he could do to change things.

At recess Pat is sitting by herself. Pat wants someone to play with. All the other kids are busy playing sports. She feel excluded. Pat doesn't know what to do. Pat feel lonely.

Eric plays alone almost everyday at school. He would like to play more with the group—sometimes. One day Eric asks if he can play. The group says: "No, you can't play. There are just enough players now. We have all the players we need."

Bob is assigned to work on a project with Ted and Bill. Ted and Bill are good friends. They play together a lot at school. So when they start to work on the project, they talk mostly to each other. They don't listen to Bob or ask his opinion. When he tries to bring up an idea, they ignore or cut him off. One time when he says something they laugh at him and call him retard.

Lisa is a new girl in her class. She is quiet and a little shy. She's been just watching the others play at recess and really wanting to be part of the group, but she's not sure how they feel about her. And, she's not sure about how to get in with them.

Independence–Dependence Stories

Once there were three really good friends named Jack, Max, and Elliot. They had been friends for quite a few years. This year Elliot suddenly started to draw away from Jack and Max and play with other people. Sometimes Elliot even was mean to Jack and Max making them feel that they had done something to hurt him. Jack and Max felt really confused. They didn't understand why Elliot was moving away from them and why he was mean to them sometimes. They didn't want to lose his friendship, but they didn't know what to do.

Jill and Alice are really good friends. They usually eat lunch together and play on the jungle gym at recess. Sometimes other kids join them, but Jill really doesn't like that. She would rather play with Alice by herself. When Alice is not in school, Jill is kind of lost. She wonders by herself at lunch break. But when Jill is out, Alice usually joins another group to play. One time after Jill had been out sick for several days, Alice wanted Jill to join her in playing with the group she had been playing with while Jill was out. Jill was upset. She thought that Alice should just play with her because they were best friends.

Terry and Pat have a lot of fun together at school. Sometimes Pat can get carried away though and do some crazy things. He does things that can get them into trouble. Terry isn't sure what to do. He wants to play with Pat but he doesn't want to get into trouble.

Bill and Tim were pals. They often got together during recess to play chess. In the middle of the year a new boy named John came to their school. John enjoyed playing soccer at his old school and every once in a while would get Bill and Tim to play with him during recess. Bill wasn't really interested in soccer and tried to persuade Tim not to play when John suggested it. Tim felt torn between Bill and John. He still enjoyed playing chess with Bill but sometimes wanted to play soccer with John.

Jill and Patti were really good friends. They lived on the same block and played with their Barbie dolls together almost every Saturday. Lisa moved into the neighborhood and started to play with Jill and Patti. She liked to play computer games and got the girls to play that once in a while. Jill really didn't like to play on the computer much, but Patti sometimes liked to do that. When Lisa suggested it, Jill tried to get Patti to say no and play with her instead. Patti felt torn. She didn't want to hurt Jill, but she sometimes wanted to play something different with someone else.

Ryan and Amin were very good friends. They relied on each other for support. In second grade, they were inseparable. They ended up in the same third-grade class. Mike was also in the same class, and became friends with Amin. Mike didn't like Ryan and tried to pull Amin away. Amin and Ryan began to argue about who to play with at recess. Ryan didn't like the same things as Mike, but Amin did.

Jessica and Halie have been in the same class in first, second, and third grade. They play together at school and at home. In October of third grade, Jessica was invited by Megan (another girl in class) to be her partner in a peer buddy program. Megan and Jessica now left the room twice a week for a short time to be peer buddies to children with special needs. Jessica enjoyed getting to know Megan. Jessica wanted the three of them to play together. Unfortunately, Halie wanted to play with Jessica alone and Megan wanted to play with Jessica without Halie.

Eileen has been friends with Jeanette for a long time. Now Eileen has met Sam. She's spending less time with Jeanette and more time with Sam. Jeanette is confused about what is going on. Jeanette is starting to feel a little left out.

Expressive–Protective Hypothetical Stories

Sam and Pat are good friends. They play together at school and at home. They usually have a lot of fun, except for one problem. Sam can lose her temper pretty easily if something doesn't go her way. When she gets mad, the play just sort of stops or Pat lets Sam have her way. One time when it happened, Pat decided that she had to do something. She wanted Sam as a friend, but she really didn't like it when Sam lost her temper.

Jerry and Bobby have been pretty good friends at school. One day at recess they have a disagreement. When it's time to go inside they are still angry at each other. They never get a chance to talk any more that day. The next day at school, Bobby tells everyone that Jerry is mean and bossy and that they shouldn't play with Jerry.

Lee and Sam spend a lot of time together. They really enjoy sharing ideas. They like to talk about how different things work and stuff that is happening at school. They also like to talk about their favorite movies and books. But once in awhile Lee comes to school feeling down and depressed. Sometimes things happen at home, like his mom really getting mad at him and he feels upset. He would like to talk to Sam about these problems but he is not sure that he should.

Bob and Jeff are good friends. They play together a lot at school and at home. The only problem is that Bob loses his temper if he doesn't get his way when they play. One time when it happened, Jeff decided that he had to do something. He wanted Bob as a friend, but really didn't like it when he always lost his temper.

Lisa made friends with the girls and started to play with Jill and Patti almost every day at recess. She really liked them both a lot. There was only one problem though. Jill could sometimes be kind of bossy. She liked to tell Patti and Lisa what to do and how to play. One day, Patti and Lisa got really mad when Jill told them what to do. They really liked her but they didn't like her bossing them around. They really wanted to do something about it.

Lindsey and Natalie were good friends. They played together at school and often went to each other's homes after school. Lindsey talked about very mature things that made Natalie feel uncomfortable. Natalie wanted to tell Lindsey not to talk about certain topics, but knew that Lindsey would get upset.

Jessica and Sara played together often at school and occasionally at home. They were both very dramatic and imaginative and enjoyed making up games together. Sara tended to dress in a younger (or babyish) way at times. She liked to wear a particular Pocahontas shirt and dressed in a fairy costume on Halloween. After everyone changed into his or her costumes, Jessica whispered to Sara that her costume was really babyish and Sara should "think about getting a new one." Sara cried throughout the rest of the Halloween festivities.

Amy and Sue have been friends for a while. Lately Sue always has to be better than Amy is. Amy is getting upset and fed up with it.

Instrumentality–Affection Hypothetical Stories

Alex and Chris often like to play computer games together after school at Chris' house. One day at lunch, Chris mentioned to Alex that his game was broken and that they couldn't get it fixed for awhile. The next day when Chris asked Alex to come over, Alex hesitated. And then Alex said that he wasn't going to come because he wanted to play computer games so he was going to see if he could go to Marty's house to play. Chris felt upset and confused. He wanted to play with Alex, but wasn't sure what to do.

Fran and Paula liked to work together in class. Fran was a good reader. She helped Paula understand words and ideas that were difficult in reading. Paula was good in math. She knew all her facts really well and liked to think about the story problems. She usually helped Fran with these. So they shared the things they were really good at with each other. One day Beth was having trouble with math work. She came to Paula for help and got a lot of help. Beth started coming back everyday, trying to be friendly but always asking for help. Paula started to get tired of it. Helping Beth didn't feel the same as helping Fran, but Paula wasn't sure what to do.

Betty and Sue are good friends at school. One day Betty promised to help Sue sell cookies at the bake sale after school. Tammy ran into Betty when she was on her way and talked her into going to play volleyball in the gym instead. When Sue saw Betty the next day, she asked her what happened. Beth lied and said her mom called and she had to go home. Just then Tammy walked by and said, "Wasn't volleyball fun yesterday after school? Want to do it again?" Betty felt really embarrassed and awkward. Sue got really mad.

Adam and Chris play together after school. They always play Nintendo at Chris' house. One day, Chris mentions that the Nintendo game is broken and can't be fixed. The next day, Chris invites Adam over after school. Adam says he's sorry, but he'd rather go to Bill's house because his Nintendo is not broken.

Ali and Samantha play together after school. They always play Nintendo at Samantha's house. One day, Samantha mentions that the Nintendo game is broken and can't be fixed. The next day, Samantha invites Ali over after school. Ali says she's sorry, but she'd rather go to Mary's house because her Nintendo is not broken.

David had a briefcase full of Beanie Babies. Zack didn't have very many so he would play with David and his Beanies at recess. When the weather became cold and damp, David stopped bringing his Beanie Babies to school. Whenever he asked Zack to play, Zack would say no, and would play with other children.

Jane and Sue sat next to each other in class. Sue asked Jane for help regularly when she did not understand directions or was confused about her work. Jane like Sue and enjoyed helping her with her schoolwork. On the playground, Sue always played with a group of girls from another class. Jane tried to join in several times but Sue made no effort to include her. Jane felt badly and didn't know what to do.

Harry wants to use Chris' vortex ball so he is real nice to him all day.

TEMPLATE FOR GROUP-RECORDING NOTES

STORY:

WHY DO THINGS LIKE THIS HAPPEN?

-
-
-
-
-
-
-
-
-

CHOICES:

-
-
-
-
-
-
-

TABLE B.3

Quality Discussion Rubric

Quality	Not Yet Observed	Emerging	Frequently Evident	Ongoing
Children make comments that connect to other children				
Children question each other				
Children listen to each other				
Children respond to each other				
Balance of teacher and child talk				
Children stay on topic and develop a shared idea				
Goals of discussion are clear to all				
Children stay on topic and develop a shared idea				

TABLE B.4

Quality of Child Explanations—Definitions

No Explanation	Simply stating that such events just happen ("people are just that way").
Character Interpretations	References to character thoughts, feelings, traits, and mental states ("Alex is greedy"; "Alex doesn't want to go to Chris' because his computer is broken.").
Circumstances	References to events or people outside of the main characters' relationship ("Alex doesn't have a computer"; "Alex may have had a date already to play computers.").
Character Differences	References to differences in opinion, views, and personality of characters ("Alex is a computer freak, Chris is not"; "They want different things.").
Character Interactions	References to history of actions and reactions ("Alex might have hogged the computer and Alex didn't want to hurt her feelings, so she's secretly glad its broken.").
Relationship	References to qualities of the relationship as a whole ("When they played they had fun, but without the computer they weren't such good friends"; "They are computer friends only.").
Metaphors or Personal Stories	References that provide connections to other knowledge or experience by going beyond the given story to metaphors or personal stories related to the theme ("Their friendship is like a rubberband"; "They are like sisters.").

TABLE B.5

Quality of Child Explanations—Rubric

Explanation Quality	Not Yet Evident	Emerging	Frequently Evident	Ongoing
Refers to one character, description, or interpretation				
Refers to circumstances				
Refers to differences between characters				
Refers to character interactions				
Refers to relationship as a whole				

Discussion Reflection Tool

Name: Date:

Questions to reflect on the quality of the process:

- Did children make comments that connect to other
    children's comments?
- Did children generate novel ideas?
- Did children question each other?
- Did children listen to each other?
- Did children respond to each other?
- Was there a good balance of teacher and child talk?
- Did children stay on topic and develop it?
- Did the goals of discussion seem clear to all?

Comments–Reflections:

Questions to reflect on the quality of the content:
- How did the children seem to understand the tension?
- What was the nature or sophistication of their explanations?
- What was the nature or sophistication of their choices?
- What kind of personal stories did they tell?
- What surprised you about their experience and their
    interpretations?

Comments–Reflections

TABLE B.6
Teacher Prompts—Definitions

Management Prompts	Prompts that focus on classroom management and calling on students.
Process Prompts	Prompts the students about the process: What is the problem?, Why do things like this happen?, and What are some choices?
Restating Student's Ideas Prompts	Prompts that restate the students' ideas and clarifies their comments.
Elaboration Prompts	Prompts that specifically pursue ideas stated by the children.
Concept Prompts	Prompts that explore big ideas, refer to the dialectic tensions, or both. Prompts that extend the students' thinking beyond the story.

TABLE B.7
Teacher Prompts—Matrix

Problem-Solving Discussion Knowledge

Competence	*Observes Model*	*With Coaching*	*Fading Support*	*Independent*
Articulates process questions				
Differentiates phases w/students				
Restates student comments				
Prompts students to elaborate				
Prompts concepts–tensions				
Prompts connections between whys and choices				
Notes qualitative differences in the whys				

CONCEPTUAL PROMPTS BY TENSION

Judgment–Acceptance

- Is there ever a time to judge your friends? What would that be like?
- What's a good friend?
- How do you know when you're friends with someone?

Independence–Dependence

- Is there a time to be independent in a friendship? What would that be like?
- Have you ever been tired of a friend?
- Can you be close friends with someone who you don't see every day?

Expressive–Protective

- Is it possible to point out something negative about a friend in a nice way?
- If you never tell them, the thing that bothers you, if you just ignore it, what do you think happens to the friendship?
- Do you ever find it hard to tell a friend something you don't like that they are doing?
- How can fights help a friendship?
- Do you ever find it hard to tell a friend something you don't like that they are doing?

Instrumentality–Affection

- Is it ever possible to show too much affection? What would that be like?
- Is there ever a time for a friendship to just be about the game or the activity you're involved in together? What would that be like?
- Can friendship be limited to one kind of activity (e.g., football friends) or place (e.g., camp friends)?

Appendix C
The Role Play Process

Role Playing Framework

Role Taking	Role Playing	Role Creating
• Building communication and dialogue skills	• Utilizing worksheets	• Improvising
• Building dialogue-writing skills	• Scaffolding spontaneity	
• Reducing performance anxiety	• Focusing on the conflict rather than the resolution	
• Strengthening relational understanding	• More teacher involvement in the action	
• Modeling audience expectations		
• Providing guidelines for student inquiry		

ROLE PLAY: QUESTIONS FOR GUIDANCE

Basic Questions

- What did they do?
- What was the choice being portrayed?
- What would happen next?

Questions for When the Students Have Been Introduced to the Tensions More Explicitly

- How does this role play relate to the tension?
- Which character(s) was experiencing the tension? How?
- Were the characters experiencing the tension differently?
- Do you think the resolution would really work?
- What did they do?
- What was the choice being portrayed?
- What would happen next?

TABLE C.1
Role Play Worksheet

Character's name	
How does he or she feel?	
Why does he or she feel that way?	
How did he or she show his or her feelings?	
What might have been a better way to express himself or herself?	
What can he or she do now to change the situation?	

Appendix D
Reflections and Connections

Conceptual-Connections Framework

Child Language   Tensions

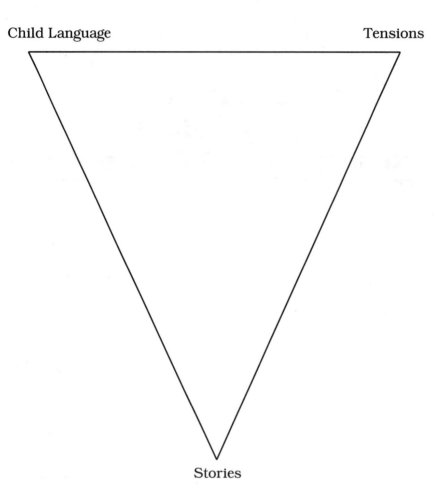

Stories

TABLE D.1
Story-Sort Chart

Old Story	New Story Match	Key Words "Children's Language"	Tension Labels
Judgement–Acceptance Story	Novel J–A Story		Judgment–Acceptance
Expressive–Protective Story	Novel E–P Story		Expressive–Protective
Independent–Dependent Story	Novel I–D Story		Independence–Dependence
Instrumentality–Affection Story	Novel I–A Story		Instrumentality–Affection

Note: Highlighted segments are displayed on the board prior to sorting activity. Novel stories and tensions are added at the appropriate time. This is done one story at a time and then adding the tension. Child language is filled in as students share their ideas.

JUDGMENT–ACCEPTANCE CIRCLE MAP

Bob, Ted, and Bill's Story

- Birds of a feather, flock together
- Alone
- Needs a friend
- Nothing has everything good, there is always something bad
- Rights or wrongs

Judgment–Acceptance Tension

INDEPENDENCE–DEPENDENCE CIRCLE MAP

Jill, Molly, and Ellen's Story

- Friendship is like a rubberband
- Expecting someone to be there
- Counting on a friend
- Needing your friend
- Free to decide about friendships

Independence–Dependence Tension

EXPRESSIVE–PROTECTIVE CIRCLE MAP

Sam and Pat's Story

- Telling a white lie
- Exploding
- Having an argument
- But is a strong word
- Speak up for yourself
- Take charge of your mind
- The nerve got away from her
- You can't say something mean in a nice way

Expressive–Protective Tension

INSTRUMENTALITY–AFFECTION CIRCLE MAP

Alex and Chris's Story

- The friendship is an illusion
- Fake friendship
- Turned his back on the friend
- Being used
- Sometimes people get sick of one another
- Got caught up playing
- It's just about the game
- The rubberband is a rope

Instrumentality–Affection Tension

Appendix E
Real Conflict

LEVELS OF RELATIONSHIP FRAMEWORK

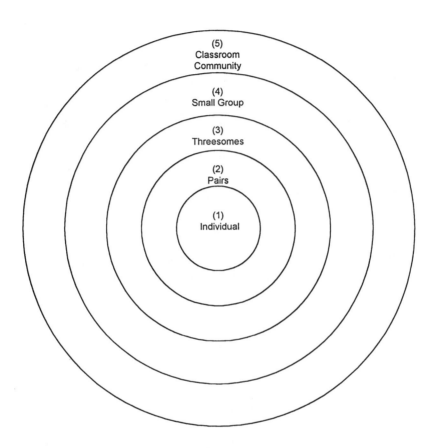

(5)
Classroom
Community

(4)
Small Group

(3)
Threesomes

(2)
Pairs

(1)
Individual

STEPS IN SOLVING REAL CONFLICTS

Step 1: Choosing Problems to Address

- Is the conflict drawing too much attention away from normal classroom-learning processes?
- How many individuals does it involve?
- How significant is the conflict to the individuals involved?
- How significant is the conflict to the healthy functioning of the community?
- Is a child or children suffering greatly as a result of this conflict?
- What kind of issues might come up if the conflict is explored?
- Which issues do I think are most important to my students' growth?
- Which issues am I most comfortable in addressing? What are my own beliefs and biases on the potential issues? How clear are they to me?
- Have other similar conflicts been occurring?
- What are the wishes and interests of the children's parents?
- Are my students and I comfortable and confident with the process?

Step 2: Choosing Who Needs to Be Involved

- Who is involved in the conflict?
- Who could benefit by participating in the RLC process?
- What are the confidentiality concerns?

Step 3: Writing a Story

- Children write the story
- Teacher write the story
- Parent–Child write story

Step 4: Engaging in the Problem-Solving Process

- What is the problem?
- Why is this happening?
- What are some choices?

Author Index

175

Subject Index